the DOOR to INNER HAPPINESS

the DOOR to INNER HAPPINESS

········

*Secrets from Around the World
for When Everything's Going Wrong*

New York Times bestselling authors
JANET BRAY ATTWOOD
& CHRIS ATTWOOD

Bestselling author in Japan
TOYOKAZU TSURUTA

AND OTHER CONTRIBUTING AUTHORS

NEW YORK

LONDON • NASHVILLE • MELBOURNE • VANCOUVER

the DOOR to INNER HAPPINESS

Secrets from Around the World for When Everything's Going Wrong

Published in New York, New York, by Morgan James Publishing. Morgan James is a trademark of Morgan James, LLC. www.MorganJamesPublishing.com

Morgan James BOGO™

A **FREE** ebook edition is available for you or a friend with the purchase of this print book.

CLEARLY SIGN YOUR NAME ABOVE

Instructions to claim your free ebook edition:
1. Visit MorganJamesBOGO.com
2. Sign your name CLEARLY in the space above
3. Complete the form and submit a photo of this entire page
4. You or your friend can download the ebook to your preferred device

ISBN 978-1-63195-415-3 paperback
ISBN 978-1-63195-416-0 eBook
Library of Congress Control Number:
2020922556

Cover Design by:
Rachel Lopez
www.r2cdesign.com

Morgan James is a proud partner of Habitat for Humanity Peninsula and Greater Williamsburg. Partners in building since 2006.

Get involved today! Visit
MorganJamesPublishing.com/giving-back

TABLE OF CONTENTS

INTRODUCTION

"Dazed, blood splattered everywhere, sirens in the background . . ."

So begins one of the stories in this book. Stories of real, very human struggles.

"Our marriage was in crisis, and then they told me, 'Your son has autism . . .'"

Some of these stories may be shocking. All of them are illuminating.

"I stood in my backyard—mid-city, mid-winter—lighting a two-by-two-meter pile of men's clothing on fire, wearing only my best underwear, a black leather jacket, and long velour boots . . ."

You'll learn ways you can deal with crisis and come out better than when you started.

"He pushed off the blankets, climbed on top of me, and began to strangle me . . ."

From all parts of the world—Japan, Norway, Finland, Germany, Thailand, Argentina, the United States, Taiwan, China—these authors share what's common to all of us. How do you manage and make sense of life when everything's going wrong?

This book is a compilation of these authors' struggles, the lessons they've learned, and their suggestions and guidance on how you can manage and make sense of your own life. You'll learn how ancient wisdom has been applied to real-life situations. You'll discover that it's possible to come through the worst imaginable experiences and still create a life that is meaningful, that brings joy to yourself and others.

Prepare yourself to hop on a roller coaster of emotions, get ready to be inspired, and open yourself up to receive some very sage advice that could help you navigate the stormy seas of your own life.

Chapter 1

STAYING IN LOVE WHEN THE MARRIAGE IS OVER

by Janet Bray Attwood and Chris Attwood (USA)

....

I woke up, shaking all over. What time is it? 3:00 a.m. Why can't I stop shaking? I wake my wife, Janet. Bleary-eyed, she takes one look at me and tells me to start taking deep breaths. "Isn't this hyperventilating?" I think as she encourages me to take deep breath after deep breath. After about 30 of these, it becomes painful.

"You got up and ran across the room," she tells me. I have no memory of that or anything else that happened in the last hour. Whatever happened, it seems to have worked.

This was a wake-up call for me. I was under tremendous pressure at work. I'd discovered that it was costing us more to place the therapists my company brought from overseas than we were charging the companies who hired them. Our cash had dwindled to zero. My partner and I barely made payroll the previous week with nothing left to pay ourselves. We couldn't even pay our payroll taxes.

That shaking morning was me coming face-to-face with the reality that I can't control what happens in my life, no matter how hard I try. In fact, the more I try, the more things spin out of control. And it was a morning when the deep love between Janet and me was tangible.

It's wonderful when love happens—and what's so wonderful for a moment should be even greater for an hour, for a day, or for a whole lifetime, right? Maybe that's why, as the song says, "Love and marriage go together like a horse and carriage." Yet for a very large number of couples, the dream of a loving and fulfilled marriage ends in a rude awakening. Not only does the ecstasy of love vanish, but it's often replaced by deep anger and even hatred.

As in Hans Christian Andersen's story of the Princess and the Pea, negative perceptions, beliefs, and judgments about the person you care for—or *once* cared for—become layered like mattresses on the tender pea of your love. The layers of negativity keep piling on, higher and higher, until you can't even feel the pea anymore. Actually, the pea is still there, but now it's beyond your perception. You're certain that love is dead and gone.

If love is a miracle, the disappearance of love is a genuine tragedy. But as you'll discover, love *can* go on. Love can continue through the end of a marriage or a long-standing relationship, and it can even grow deeper and stronger. While the euphoria of new love may not be a feeling that can last forever, it can be replaced by emotions that are every bit as wonderful and much less fragile. Love does not have to be the story of "Paradise Lost." Through all the transitions that life imposes on us, you really can perpetuate the love you feel for another person, both within and outside of marriage.

The keys to staying in love can be expressed in just a few words. But this fact can be deceptive. In less than an hour, a great violinist could "tell" you how to play the instrument, but that wouldn't make you ready to go out and play.

Any really worthwhile endeavor is a process first of discovery, then understanding, and, finally, action. No amount of talking can match the actual experience of playing that violin.

This book is the story of learning how to turn catastrophe into growth and, ultimately, into a fulfilling life. Our contribution is the story of how, after five years of the most challenging of marriages, we've forged a bond so deep and so rich that it survives and thrives more than 20 years after our divorce.

But to understand the lessons we've learned and how you can apply them in your own life, we have to go back to where it all started . . .

Chris and Janet Goin' to the Chapel

We're in love! We've found our soul mate and we're getting married! We're going to get a house together and have a family. We'll support each other and share our hopes and dreams. We'll help each other through the rough spots and teach our children to be good, honest, responsible adults.

We'll have great sex and take romantic getaways. We'll get to cuddle on the sofa whenever we want and cherish each other for the rest of our lives. We'll protect each other and we'll have a partner to help us achieve our dreams.

Oh, and the wedding! We're only doing this once, so it's got to be incredible. We'll invite all our friends, and everything will be perfect. We'll have the support of all our family and friends and begin our life together with the most romantic of honeymoons!

We were engaged for six months. Both of us had been married before, but Janet had never had a big, formal wedding. So, ours was going to be the fulfillment of all her dreams.

For weeks, we planned all the elements of the wedding. Invitations went out, food and flowers were ordered, the wedding dress was picked out, we bought a house with help from Chris' mom, all the arrangements were made. We wrote our vows and practiced the wedding ceremony. Friends and family flew in from around the country.

We even consulted a Vedic astrologer to find an auspicious day to begin this new phase of our lives. As he gave us our date, he said, "Anything begun on this day will never decay."

The date arrived and it was glorious—a perfect spring day. We began it with a special ceremony in our house for friends and family. Janet was radiant and gorgeous. Chris was beaming. Both of us were floating on air.

That afternoon we went to the church where 300 of our friends greeted us. Janet had fine-tuned the wedding to the smallest detail. It began with 30 schoolgirls coming down the aisle two by two, followed by Janet's five bridesmaids. Each bridesmaid carried a candle, which she placed beside the altar of the church. Finally, Janet entered, wearing the most beautiful wedding dress in the world.

Chris recalls the moment: "I remember watching Janet come down the aisle, and she was an absolute angel of love, radiating joy. She stopped several times, and her eyes were filled with such incredible warmth as she saw some dear, beloved friend who was present to share this special moment with her. She showered her love on everyone in that chapel and the feeling was sublime."

The service itself was filled with wonder. Years afterward, people were still telling us what an amazing, deeply moving experience the wedding had been. Our dear friend Maryanne sang, the schoolgirls added a beautiful, heart-wrenching song, and several of our friends read inspiring passages, including this one from Maharishi Mahesh Yogi's "Love and God:"

> *"Love is the sweet expression of life, it is the supreme content of life. Love is the force of life, powerful and sublime. The flower of life blooms in love and radiates love all around it.*
>
> *"Life expresses itself through love. The stream of life is a wave on the ocean of love, and life is expressed in the waves of love, and the ocean of love flows in the waves of life.*
>
> *"What a comfort love brings to the heart. The heart tickles with the thought of love. The heart tickles with the thought of love and waves of life begin to roll on the ocean of love.*
>
> *"Every wave of life is full with the ocean of love."*

After the wedding, we all went to a nearby park for our outdoor reception, took pictures with the families, danced, ate, and made merry. When all our friends had gone home and we returned to our new house, we found our living room piled three feet high with presents. So, what could we do? We spent the next three hours, sitting on the floor, opening present after present after present.

Talk about Christmas! This was the Christmas to end all Christmases—the beginning of our dream life together. We knew there would be ups and downs, but we also knew that our love would get us through whatever lay ahead. We would build a life together, have children, share our thrills and our disappointments, cuddle together in the evenings, enjoy great fulfillment in bed whenever we wanted, go on wonderful trips, and have a partner who would always be there for us. We knew that any tough times would only render our love even more wonderful, as we made it through them together. Wasn't that the story we'd watched at the movies since we were kids?

You probably saw that movie too . . .

That Was Then, This is Now

Today, we're no longer married. Thinking back on our wedding and the happiness we felt, there's naturally some sadness associated with the transitions we've been through. But though our connection is no longer a romantic or physical one, the bond we share is deeper and more profound than ever.

How can this be? Or . . . how could it be otherwise? We married because we felt a deep love for each other. The truth is, *that didn't change*. It became hidden behind a great deal of hurt and misunderstanding. And though our love's expression has changed, we've definitely been able to rediscover it. We've each come to realize that the hurt we've felt had nothing to do with the other person. It had only to do with ourselves.

We are not unique in any way, except that we decided that learning, growing, and loving was more important than whatever form our relationship took. What we discovered is that our love became the most incredible, rewarding experience we could imagine. Our big aha was that it didn't matter how we showed up in each other's life. The important thing was that the love remained.

What would it mean to discover how to stay "in love" all of the time, not just with your partner (or your ex-partner), but *all of the time*? What if you could have the joy of love even if your partner doesn't seem willing to meet you in that loving place?

Love is an abstract concept describing the feeling that draws us together. To truly love is to want for another their complete joy and fulfillment in life—no matter what your relationship with them may look like. In other words, "I want for you what you want for you."

Ultimately, the love you feel for others is just the love you feel for yourself. The anger, hurt, or distress you feel toward others are those feelings you have about yourself reflected back to you. The mistake the intellect makes is to think that what you feel has anything to do with anyone else.

The reality is that our world is as we are. When you feel pain, hurt, anger, or upset toward someone else, these feelings are the signal that there is something in you that needs to be healed.

Your emotional body functions in a way that is very similar to your physical body. What do you do when you feel pain in some part of your body? If you break your arm, do you tell your arm, "You shouldn't hurt me. You're being unkind to me. You should stop making me feel this pain." Of course not.

When you feel pain in your physical body, it's because there is something that needs attention. When you feel pain in your emotional body, it's for the same reason. You can blame someone else for your pain, and feel separated and suffer, or you can realize that this pain is a gift to help you heal and step up to another level of loving.

Does that mean you should grin and bear it when you hurt? No. Sometimes you need to take time to yourself, allow the pain to diminish, in order to open your heart and mind to the healing.

Will you want to remarry your divorced partner? Not necessarily. Love can take many forms. Love is about acceptance of what is, in yourself and in another person. You can love and accept another without approving of their actions or continuing to make them part of your life.

Expansion and Contraction . . . Nature's Guidance System

The concept of expansion and contraction is an easy way to describe the internal movement of the emotions we experience in relationships. Without realizing that this movement, in and out, is the key to staying in "flow," most people find themselves struggling through life. What does it mean to expand or to contract?

Think about how you might describe your feelings when you are expanded. Many people would say expanded means feeling happy, joyful, open, light, excited, turned on, ready for anything, compassionate, loving, caring, generous, thoughtful, considerate . . .

And how does it feel when you're contracted? Maybe shut down, closed off, in pain, dark, angry, sad, disappointed, frustrated, jealous, overcome with grief, worried, anxious, tense, uptight, shrunken, depressed . . .

Both expansion and contraction are natural parts of life. We see them even in the cycles of nature. During the day, it's light. There is an expansion of activity, increased interaction, and things open up (flowers, businesses, people). At night, it's dark, things shut down, most people and animals rest, and the activity becomes less.

In nature, we know that these cycles of rest and activity are part of life. One is not better or worse than the other. Yet, in our relationships, contraction is generally associated with pain. None of us wants to experience pain, so we do everything we can to avoid the contraction phase of our relationships.

And yet, for all our attempts to avoid it, here it comes again. Expansion and contraction are natural parts of life. We all expand and contract every day. This book is about learning to embrace both. In this chapter, we'll share a simple process for moving through contraction easily, gently, and with full responsibility so that you can return to the wonderful delights of expansion as quickly and as often as possible.

You begin to transform your life when you begin to take responsibility for your own happiness. To think there is anyone else but you who is responsible for your hurt, for your unhappiness, for your suffering, is to live in delusion. You are the responsible party. The good news is: Entering back into love depends on no one but you.

So, you've made the choice to stay in love, no matter what the outcome may be, but how the heck do you do that? It sounds great. The challenge comes when you're faced with a partner who is driving you nuts. For most of us, it's a great achievement not to bite their head off, much less be loving. And have you noticed that when you try to be loving and you don't feel loving, that doesn't work either? In fact, it usually makes things worse.

Fortunately, once you understand what happens when you "fall out of love" (or contract), coming back to love (to expansion) is simple, effortless, and natural. That doesn't mean it's altogether fun. The process of releasing emotional pain means "stepping into the fire of your own discomfort," consciously choosing to fully experience the emotions as they come up. In the following section, we'll share with you how to do that in a gentle way in order to allow yourself to move through the process of releasing the emotions, nurturing yourself until the emotions have passed, and then communicating your needs, desires, and preferences clearly to your partner.

The Expansion Process

The Expansion Process we describe here, and the tools to help you expand, are drawn from our ebook, *From Sad to Glad: 7 Steps to Facing Change with Love and Power*. This process can apply to any relationship—an ex-spouse, a wife or husband, a child, a dear friend, a mother or father, a sister or brother, a boss, a coworker, or any other relationship. We will use the term "partner" throughout this chapter to refer to any person with whom you feel contracted.

So, what happens when you contract? Something is said or not said, something is done or not done, that infuriates you, or disappoints you, or saddens you, or upsets you in some way. When this happens, here is the process for returning to expansion as quickly as possible:

Step #1: Notice. When you get upset, become conscious that you are contracted. Ask yourself, "Am I expanded or am I contracted?"

Step #2: Breathe. When we are upset, we tend to take shallow breaths, or even stop breathing. Take a deep breath to open the physiology, which will help open up your emotions as well.

Step #3: Ask to Be Open. Remind yourself that you want to expand, to open up again. If it's helpful, just say quietly inside, "Please help me to expand, to be able to be open again."

Step #4: Go into the Feeling. Give yourself time and space to feel the emotions that are coming up. The emotions need the chance to come out. Do this privately. Don't take out your anger, or your grief, or your upset on your partner, no matter how much you think they may deserve it.

Step #5: Feel the Body. As you allow the emotions to come out, notice any area in your body where you feel any sensations. Remember that sickening feeling when someone just ripped your guts out? That's contraction. The sensation could also be some tightness, or constriction, or heat, or tingling, or any other kind of sensation. Allow your attention to go to that area. Just continue feeling that sensation until you notice it is gone or almost gone.

Step #6: Use the Tools. Once the intensity of emotions is mostly gone, use your tools to expand again. A tool is anything you know from experience will help you expand again. Typically, this involves a state change. You're working on a project and can't come up with any new ideas. Take a walk to change from a mental to a physical state. Some really bad news arrives, take time to pray, meditate, or be in nature, changing from an emotional state to a spiritual state. You're confused about how to move forward, worried about your bills. Take time to write out the vision for your life, create a spreadsheet with all your income and expenses and projected new income, list the things you can do to move forward, changing from an emotional state to a mental state.

When you're contracted is a time to be gentle with yourself. It's okay to be tender, and it's okay to take time to nurture yourself. You deserve it and you need it right now.

Step #7: Communicate Clearly. When you are feeling open again, communicate your needs, desires, and preferences to your partner in a way that expresses the whole truth: both your love and appreciation of them, along with what you need or want them to change.

All seven steps of The Expansion Process could happen in less than 5 minutes, or they could take several days. When you feel pain, upset, and other forms of contraction, these are signals that something needs your attention. These seven steps are the way you give yourself that attention. These steps are what it means to treat yourself with love and compassion. Staying in love with yourself is the prerequisite to staying in love with anyone else. Practicing these steps can transform your life.

Staying in love is about learning to love unconditionally. "I love you no matter what you do, no matter where you go, no matter what happens in either of our lives." Such love is only possible when you have gotten to the point of knowing your happiness, your success, your fulfillment in life depends only on you. And, that's the good news!

Janet Bray Attwood and Chris Attwood *are co-authors of the* New York Times *bestsellers* The Passion Test *and* Your Hidden Riches. *They arranged 70% of the interviews for the movie and book,* The Secret, *and have played a key role in many of the alliances in the transformational industry. Together they have trained more than 3,500*

Passion Test facilitators in more than 65 countries so that The Passion Test has been taken by over 1,000,000 people worldwide and has become the #1 tool for discovering passion and purpose throughout the world. Janet has homes in Italy and Fairfield, Iowa, although she is traveling, teaching, and mentoring most of the time. Chris and his wife, Doris, with their three children, split time between Fairfield, Iowa and Hannover, Germany.

Chapter 2
WHEN ALL HOPE IS LOST

by Nicco Takahashi (Japan)

....

I was floating in a place with no up or down. Something grabbed me and pulled me away. I was being pulled back down. At some point, I realized I'd re-entered my physical body, not knowing my body was in respiratory arrest.

"Back again. Not dead, again."

I came back to consciousness. I was in a hospital bed. I'd soon learn I was in intensive care.

I can't clearly recall what exactly it was that I did. I think I scrambled to find any kind of drug—from my dog's Filarioidea medicine, eye drops, and supplements to copious amounts of sleeping pills and psychotropic drugs my doctor had given me. I took them all. Whatever it took to end the pain.

That was the fourth time I had tried to kill myself since I'd become an adult. The total count of my suicide attempts had passed double digits since the first time I slit my wrists in primary school.

I only have one good memory from my childhood. Anxiety and fear hung over the rest.

On a cold night, with temperatures below zero in a wealthy area of Tokyo, I was in a room of an old house, wrapped up under the futon, holding on tight to that anxiety and fear. My father was most likely at the Pachinko gambling joint or with a woman. My mother spent most of her time at her parents. She'd been doing that ever since she realized my father was sexually abusing me. My older brother, needing some outlet to deal with his own stress from our parents, would either be at home bullying me or at his friend's house.

No money, no food, and unable to turn on the oil heater myself, I was so very cold. The only heat I found was the faint warmth of a light bulb. On the rare occasion that my father was home, whether he was drinking or not, he would throw things at his family, so our stained plaster walls were dotted with the holes made by his attacks. Though she wasn't as bad as him, my mother's mood swings were severe, and when she was in a bad mood, she would hit me and my brother.

Little noises like the steps of passers-by outside or the wind causing the house to creak were enough to frighten a nine-year-old girl left alone. I was very afraid of being alone, yet, oddly, there was a strange sense of comfort in my solitude—there was nobody there to hurt me.

"What was I born for?"

Have you ever asked yourself that question? Today I live an inspired life, graced with many blessings and a strong sense of purpose. But it wasn't always that way. This chapter is for you if you've gone through or are going through a dark time in life. I'll show you that there is hope, no matter how dark the darkness becomes, and give you some steps you can take to return to a brighter, more hopeful life.

I grew up wondering and doubting what I was born for. For a nine-year-old child, there is no place to go but home, no matter how terrible it was there. I spent a lot of time alone at home without my mother. Though I was plagued by my father's abuse, I couldn't tell anybody, and during the winter, I would sit and cry, alone in the corner of the room, wrapped under my blanket. There were days when there was no food at home, so all I ate was lunch at school.

"Why?" I'd ask myself.

Why must I be punched, forced to do what I don't want to . . . why must I be left alone, starving in the cold?

"What can I do?"

What can I do so I'm told that I'm good, that I can do it, that I did well . . . what can I do so they'd hold me and tell me they're proud?

"Is it because I'm a bad child?"

I was average-looking, no good at essays, made mistakes at calculating, a slow runner, and couldn't really draw either. So, I figured if I studied, if I stood tall, and if I could do sports and got crafty with my hands, they might love me.

I worked hard. I bit my nails, ground my teeth, and held on as much as I could. But no matter how hard I tried, how much I endured, nothing ever changed. All I had were endless tears of frustration and inadequacy.

Though I was screaming inside, no adult, not even my parents, would hear me, and eventually I became good at numbing my heart and body, pretending and getting through wherever I was without trusting anybody.

This got worse as I acted like a bright and bubbly girl at school so no one would know the abnormal situation I was facing at home. At times I would experience fits of amnesia when I would forget where my house was or what my name was.

When I suddenly came to, I might be in the middle of a test at school. I'd suddenly realize where I was and only just be writing my name while many others already finished. At times, I would find myself just lost on the grounds of my neighborhood shrine at night. At times like that, I would think of "him."

The Best Day of My Life

It was a crisp autumn day with clear blue skies when a global superstar visited our school. He was sparkling with a bright light, more powerful than the sun, from his head to his toes. He would hug and say, "I love you!" to every single student who followed and clung to him. I kept my distance, unable to get near him on my own, so I hid behind everybody else. Still, he noticed, and with his arms wide open he said, "Come on!" and I jumped right into his arms.

He was warm.

He was kind.

I was held, and I could finally breathe.

"We are family!"

This was Michael Jackson. The King of Pop. Those words and that hug saved me. I felt overwhelmed and my eyes filled with tears.

But those tears were different from the ones I had cried in sadness. This was the first time in my life that I felt safe and glad to be alive. Even as I look back now, I believe that this was the first time I had ever felt happy about existing on this earth.

Whenever I would experience difficulty, I would think back to those words and Michael's hug. And each time, I could feel a beacon of hope shine down into the loneliness that surrounded me.

In spite of that wonderful moment, I was still unstable. Over the course of my life, I've been diagnosed with 11 different mental illnesses.

As soon as I got a job in high school, I moved out of the torture chamber of my family's house. I was still playing the charade of a "good, normal girl" and the girl who wanted to be somewhere else; both still didn't feel like the real me.

Even after I became an adult, those "two mes" continued to exist. There was me who was a diligent office worker, trusted by others, and another me who only came out after dark. I worked in the sex industry in the evenings, dealing with the sexual desires of men. I burned through the money I earned left, right, and center. Some I donated to charity. Some I spent on things from expensive brands and the rest disappeared in drinks at a bar manned with pretty, young men.

When I finally met someone and fell in love, he already had a home with a wife and kids. On nights he wasn't around, I was all alone. I was back to being that cold and shivering, frightened little nine-year-old, lonely, and scared to death that he would leave me.

I didn't want him to throw me away. I was afraid that if I even did one thing wrong, he would leave me, so I wore clothes that he liked, ate what he wanted, and I would have sex with him whenever he asked, no matter how tired I was. I planned myself around his schedule. Showing him my smile became my everything.

One night I received a call. The woman on the other end of the line claimed that she had been his mistress for two decades. So, he, his wife, the mistress, and I sat down to talk. I watched as if I was observing a foreign world as his wife said, "It's fine as long as there are no children involved," while the mistress asked for a million yen a month (about $9,000). I felt nothing . . . and then, I broke.

I attempted suicide again and again. Every time I would fail, I thought, "Next time I must die." After taking all the drugs in my house, then being carried away in an ambulance, and miraculously recovering from respiratory arrest, I was put in a secure ward in a psychiatric hospital.

Locked Away

It was an eight-person room with iron bars over the windows. The people in my room were continuously talking to someone who wasn't there. An old lady in her 80s was in the next bed over, and every time I would ask how old she was, she would always answer, "19." She would wake up at half-past four every morning, go to the bathroom, then walk around to make sure nothing had changed. She was forever living a day that she lived back when she was 19.

Why was I put in a place like this? I was angry, devastated, and confused. Though it was a secure ward, you could walk along the hallways or visit the lobby area. But I didn't want to meet or talk to other patients or nurses, so I spent all day, every day staring at the plain, boring white ceiling.

One day, I heard someone say, "Michael Jackson is dead" down the hallway.

Michael? Dead?

That Michael who held me is dead?

Peeling my heavy body off my bed, I forced myself up and toward the lobby where the television was. I felt dizzy and weak, but that was no excuse. I clung onto the railing and crawled my way to the TV and watched as they reported on Michael Jackson's death.

The Little Mermaid

Strangely I did not feel the emotion of sadness in that moment. When I realized that I didn't even have tears to cry, I remembered the story of "The Little Mermaid" by Hans Christian Andersen. The mermaids did not cry because they didn't have tears. They had a lifespan of 300 years, yet they disappeared into a bubble when they died.

The truth is that human beings with hearts are the ones who have eternal souls. That desire for love is why the Little Mermaid searched for an eternal soul and was willing to lose her voice and everything else to win the prince's love.

The story describes how every time the mermaid would walk, every step was full of pain as if she was being stabbed with a knife. Yet she managed to dance like no one had ever seen before with a smile on her face. No matter how much she loved him, she couldn't tell the prince, nor could she tell him that she was the one who had saved him.

When I read this story, I thought, "I'm just like that mermaid."

To gain that "eternal soul," the story suggests that someone must love you. To get that love from another, the mermaid gives all of herself and even sacrifices herself for the one she loves. The mermaid doesn't think about the consequences. She takes action without thought just to be loved by her prince.

When I was a child, unloved by my parents, and when I was betrayed by the married man who I loved and gave my all to, I felt like an emotionless mermaid, searching for something to support my strange, damaged self. I was so afraid of being thrown away, I had to hold on to something to survive.

But did you know that there is more to the story after the mermaid turned into bubbles?

The Daughter of Air

The mermaid rose up into the sky and became a "daughter of air." Her purpose became being one with the wind to bring cool breezes to the people in hot countries, to cheer people up with the smell of flowers, and to do good. After doing good for 300 years, she finally gains that eternal soul.

After Michael Jackson's death, I decided that I want to be a "daughter of air." I want to breathe life into other mermaids, that, like me, have low self-esteem and trap themselves in broken relationships. This has given my life a sense of purpose and meaning. Just as Michael Jackson made me feel glad to be alive for the first time when he visited my school.

I know what it is like to be stuck in a cycle of physical and mental pain. And I know firsthand how hard it is to live while hiding your truth. But I also know what freedom and relief feel like when you finally cut yourself loose from those things.

No matter what you have been through, no matter how hopeless you may feel, there is a special and unique purpose for which you were born. When you discover that, you, too, can become a "daughter of air" and create a life that gives you deep fulfillment.

To help you on your way, let me share with you the "Mermaid Complex." There are three fundamental traits of a mermaid.

Mermaid Trait #1

The mermaid's first trait is her inability to stand on her own two feet. Mermaids don't have an independent sense of self. They become codependent due to a lack of income or because they worry more about others and others' feelings so that they forget about their own needs.

Mermaid Trait #2

The mermaid's second trait is that just like the mermaid in the story who exchanged her voice for legs, she has difficulty communicating. She doesn't know how to speak up for herself and instead bottles her emotions up to get approval from others.

Mermaid Trait #3

Lastly, mermaids feel like they are living in the wrong world. The Little Mermaid lives in a beautiful castle under the sea, yet she dreams of living on land with humans, even before she meets the prince. If you've suffered from bullying or abuse, you'll tend to have a disconnect between your heart and your physical body. You feel that you don't belong, and nothing brings you joy.

The Mermaid Lessons

I made the decision to become a "daughter of air," but I was stumped about how to do that and wondered if I was to spend the rest of my life searching for happiness. There is a saying, "When the student is ready, the teacher will appear." I must have been ready because at this time I met my mentor, Janet Bray Attwood, and her tool, The Passion Test. Through discovering my passions and with help from Janet, I was able to discover my most authentic self.

For four years, I worked as Janet's assistant and visited 8 countries. I studied under her and got to touch the hearts of many around the world. Through meeting people who had lived with the same pain in their hearts, I realized that I wasn't alone and finally found some relief.

My past traumas healed little by little as I opened up to Janet and told my story in front of the world. My life and my thinking became more balanced as I learned to love myself, rather than seeking love from someone else.

All of that has helped me conceptualize the "Mermaid Lessons" below, which will help mermaids like you and me become humans with eternal souls.

1. **Leave the past in the past**: Time flows toward the future. You cannot wind it back. There's no value gained from getting mad or feeling sad about the past. All it does is build up negative feelings. Instead of being trapped in the hardships of your past, realize that the past is the past and the good news is that it's over. The past cannot be changed so looking to what you can do from here in the now is most important.

2. **Stand on your own feet**: Happiness cannot be handed to you by someone else. You must take it for yourself. You must stand on your own two feet and think for yourself. It is hard to move forward while being financially or mentally dependent on another person.

3. **Connect with someone**: Connecting with others begins with telling them your honest feelings. When you think "If I tell them, they'll think I'm weird" or "They might feel bad" then you hide away your emotions. I hope you are able to find some courage to speak your mind. It is not as scary as it might seem, and when you open your heart, you give the other person permission to open theirs to you. Relationships deepen when you speak from the heart. Joy and fun grow by sharing your feelings with others.

4. **Have passions in life**: Passion is a life force. No matter what obstacle, passion will burn it and turn into fuel to help you live your purpose. That power will never run out. Use The Passion Test to discover your top passions and then starting making choices that allow you to live those passions most fully.

5. **Accept yourself**: Everybody experiences negative emotions like anger and sadness. You can't get anything out of putting yourself down for having those emotions. Forgive yourself and it will become easier to forgive others as well.

Bit by bit, I changed my way of thinking, and I evolved. At the hospital, I refused to go out in the hallway or to communicate with others. When my thinking changed, I saw that the people there were unable to live "normally" on land and needed a place like the bottom of the ocean, the secure ward, and they were able to be kind and thoughtful of others there. No matter what I said, the nurse accepted me as I was. The iron bars on my windows that I thought were there to trap me were actually protecting me. I lived my life thinking I was strange, but I was able to reframe that thought into "I may be strange, but there's nothing wrong with that. Let me just do what I can right now."

The perimeter of my movements expanded from my bed to the whole room, then to the hallway, and I was eventually discharged and returned to society.

People say you can't choose the name your parents give you or that you can't choose your parents, but I don't believe that. I gave myself the name Nicco Takahashi. My mentor, Janet, calls me her daughter. To me, Janet is my mother. I also have a daughter on Cebu island in the Philippines. They are both my true family. Them, and my beloved, supportive husband.

As "a daughter of air," I support deeply wounded mermaids in finding themselves and their purpose through counseling and workshops. That is my life's work.

What is your life's work? Isn't it exciting to think about finding it?

I may not be able to sing and dance like Michael, but I can "Heal the World" in my very own way. That is my true purpose now.

What is your purpose? Set your intention right now to discover it and start living it. It begins with discovering your passions.

Dear Michael, I'm all grown up now.
Please watch over me as I wrap the world in love.
I love you. R.I.P.

Nicco Takahashi is a businesswoman, a counselor of young people with suicidal tendencies, a Passion Test facilitator, and a wife. Through her own efforts, with help from many others, she has transformed her life and become an inspiration to all who know her.

Chapter 3

WHEN SUCCESS IS A CATASTROPHE

By Ngor Rossikon Gangate (Thailand)

....

H ave you ever felt empty inside even though it seems like you've got everything?

Back in 2009, I got married. At the same time, I was really successful in my career as an acting coach. Every movie that I coached was a hit. I was directing, producing, and acting on a stage of my own production and I earned $15,000 a month while a bottle of water here costs only $.33 cents, so please do the math. People on social media considered me rich. It was a fabulous life, until one day.

It was almost midnight. I was lying in bed reading the next movie script that I would be coaching. Next to me, lying against my back, was my then husband. He wanted to make a movie, but he hadn't yet had any success. I giggled at the story I was reading as it was so funny (later this movie would become the number one movie in Thailand). While I was giggling, my husband turned over, pushed against me really hard, and shouted: "Be Quiet!"

I replied politely, "I AM F***ING WORKING!"

He turned to me and hit me hard on my lap and screamed, "SHUT THE F**K UP." I was always the kind of girl who would rather be killed than shut my mouth. But this time I did shut my mouth as I carefully closed my laptop nice and slow and then hit him really hard with it on his lap.

In the blink of an eye, he ripped open his blanket, jumped on top of me, put his hands around my neck, and began to squeeze. I gasped for air, but none could get past the stranglehold he had on my neck. His face turned into someone I didn't know. His eyes grew wide, his jaw was as tight as a fist, and he kept saying "Will you shut up? Will you dare say another word? Huh? Will you?"

There was a cacophony of voices in my head. "Am I gonna die? I need to fight. I'm a fighter. Is he going to kill me? Gosh, am I one of those girls who are abused by their husbands? Nooooo!"

Gathering the last power I had in me, I kicked him in the stomach, and I was free! I ran into the bathroom and locked myself in. Trying to catch my breath, my eyes were so hurting so much that I looked in the mirror to see what had happened. A vein had broken and my whole eye was bright red.

That was my wake-up call. And my final call to get on board to create another kind of life!

That horrible scene woke me up to see what was really happening in my life in every dimension. I married this guy, even though I didn't love him. But why did I marry him? I started to ask myself questions I had never asked before. I go to work where I am highly paid, but why do I get panic attacks every time? I invested $100,000 to direct my own theatre production, hoping to have some sponsors to cover the rest of the costs, but there are none. That means I will lose about $30,000, even with a full house.

Everything was going downhill while I was pretending it was alright. I cried myself to sleep many nights.

One day I was doing a press conference for my current production. One question really set me back on my heels. The reporter asked me a standard question: "Before you became so successful in your acting coach career, did you ever feel disheartened?" I was about to give him a cliché answer like, "Oh yes, of course, but I got through it, blah, blah, blah." But in my head, I tried to find the most honest answer I could give. And surprisingly I couldn't say I had felt disheartened because I hadn't! I never felt disheartened before becoming successful. So, there comes the bigger question: "WHY?"

Right after the press conference, I ran back home and used the Buddha technique for success to unwrap my success pattern. In Buddhism, there are 4 simple, yet deep, rules to help people be successful in realizing their goals. The Buddha said when you have a goal you have to pursue it with these 4 rules in mind:

1. Passion
2. Consistency
3. Focus
4. Analysis

Goals!

In Buddhism, a goal is not something you want to have by praying for it. It is something you have to do for yourself and for the good of others. I had no goal for my career when I was in my last year at university. I knew that I loved acting, but I am not that pretty by Thai standards, so that meant acting could only be my hobby.

Then one day I had the chance to coach a friend in a university theatre production and it turned out really well. With my coaching, he was able to act much better and the director praised me for helping him. When I see that I can make a useful contribution, then my self-esteem is high. So, I thought, "Wow, it would be great if I can teach what I love." I love acting and if I can help other actors by coaching them, that would be perfect!

At this time in Thailand, there was no such thing as an acting coach, yet many actors act like they need some help, so I could see there was a place for me. I was hopeful that I could pay my bills doing this. So, becoming an acting coach became my goal.

When it comes to passion in Buddhism, it doesn't necessarily mean you have to do what you love, but you have to put love into what you do. How? Curiosity. Curiosity makes life fun. One of the master monks I studied with, Arjarn Cha, gave me a great metaphor to understand this.

He said it is like planting a mango tree. You enjoy planting the tree, learning how to get it to grow, and how to protect it from dying. The way to enjoy the tree is to enjoy asking the questions that will make it grow beautifully and that is all.

But most people don't do that. They plant the tree and then look at it every day, asking "When will the tree give me mangoes?" When you keep looking for the result and forget to enjoy the process, you will get easily disheartened because you're always looking for the mangoes and, before long, you start to think that the mangoes will never come.

So, if your focus is on getting a "yes," then you're going to hear "no" far too often. But if your focus is on how to improve, then the "no" is just showing you another way to make it better and, in no time, when you look up at the tree, you see the mangos.

In that press conference, I replied honestly to the reporter and told him that I have never felt disheartened. The reporters didn't seem to believe me, so I told them, "Yes, of course, I used to feel disheartened at times. For example, when I was on the treadmill and I kept looking at the time asking myself, 'When is it going to finish?'"

Forty minutes on that treadmill seemed like forever. I had no fun doing that and right after I got off the treadmill, I'd look in the mirror hoping to see a flatter belly. But it looked exactly the same as before I worked out! So, yes, that made me feel disheartened.

Being disheartened is the cancer of success. I could never lose weight doing that. But on my acting coach thing, I never had any idea if I would love this career or not. I love acting, but teaching and coaching? I didn't know about that.

Since I knew nothing about teaching, I set myself to learn and learn. I took many acting classes to learn from the best teachers. I read tons of acting books. And the most important thing is that I never asked myself, "When am I gonna be a successful acting coach?"

I told the reporters at that press conference that I had just realized that I am successful because they had asked me this question. The seven years I spent pursuing this dream seem like the blink of an eye because I was living in the present, focused on practicing and challenging myself to be a better teacher, to help my actors. Forty minutes can feel like forever when you don't enjoy being on that treadmill and you keep asking, "When am I gonna lose this fat?" But the 3,679,200 minutes in those seven years felt like nothing when I was fully occupied in the present moment, excited, curious, learning how to become the best acting coach I could possibly be.

Now looking back to when I started this career and there was no acting coach in Thailand, it seems like a miracle. There were some acting teachers at that time, but an acting coach for movies as a real, paid position? That didn't exist.

I remember going to many directors to offer my services and none of them said yes. They told me that there is no such position. The only thing similar to what I was describing was "assistant to the director." So, I told them I can do that too as long as I can help the actors with their acting. They said, "Okay." And they would let me know when they were in need of an assistant. I didn't take it as a no; I took it as a "not yet."

While I waited for my break, I cooped myself up, reading many acting books, taking many acting classes. I worked as a casting director for TVC, the major television network in Thailand, just so I could stay close to acting as much as possible.

Then one day it happened. Some people say it was luck, while I say the luck was when this opportunity met my readiness. There was a film called *My Girl* in which the entire cast was kids and new faces. The director was new too, so he asked me to help him as an acting coach and bam! That was my first job as an acting coach.

The movie company didn't have a salary for my position, so the director gave part of his salary to me. I was paid $300 a month, but I worked like I was hired for $30,000 a month. I practiced and rehearsed with those kids almost every day. I watched, talked, thought, and even dreamed about how to make them better actors.

I analyzed my results to keep all the good stuff and adjust or get rid of all the "not working methods." The mango tree bore fruit when the movie was released and was very successful. People kept talking about the children's acting and from that time on the movie production set had an acting coach position for every movie.

That was my aha moment and the answer to all the questions I'd had about my miserable life. With my marriage, I had no goal and very low self-esteem. When my husband and I were dating, he kept asking me to marry him, and I finally said yes out of guilt. I felt guilty for not loving him, guilty for using him to make me feel good, to be able to say at least I have somebody, guilty for my bad behavior toward him and he was still there. So, I said yes because of that guilt.

At TVC, I got paid a lot, but the job led me to suffer from panic attacks. In the beginning, I enjoyed working at TVC because it was something different from movies, but after a few years went by and I didn't learn anything new, I stayed there just because of the money.

I saw my smart friends helping others improve and earning a third of what I was making, while I'm coaching women how to apply whitening lotion nicely on their skin to attract a guy with that bleached, white skin! So many times I wanted to shout to the storyboard, "C'mon why do we need to be white when we're right at the equator? We need melanin!"

But I kept my mouth shut and just did my job so I could get that nice paycheck. As a result, I had no self-respect.

For my theatre production, I focused on how to get the sponsors instead of making the production the best I possibly could. I forgot to be present and enjoy every minute with what I love and wanted to share.

As I had these realizations, I stopped everything and asked myself these 4 questions and took the time to find the answers. I encourage you to ask yourself these questions. You may find the answers surprising.

1. How can I raise my self-esteem? It is important to see what my good qualities are and use them with all my heart in order to improve myself and help others in their lives.

2. What do I really want for my life and why? So, I wrote down what my ideal life would look like.

3. What is most important in my life? I prioritized the things I love by doing The Passion Test.

4. How do I stay in the moment so I can enjoy the process instead of focusing on the result? So, I practice meditation every day to stay present and go beyond meditation by practicing Vipassana to lessen the ego's grip on me.

There's a story that once the Buddha studied the highest form of meditation with some master in India and he realized that this meditation was like a stone on the weeds. The stone makes the weeds pause their growth but doesn't kill them. In a similar way, people may feel calm while meditating but not while they are living their normal life.

He found that many people suffer from non-stop greed—even what could be considered "good greed," the greed to do good deeds. And greed occurs when we are gripped by the ego. So, to uproot the weeds, Vipassana provides a way to see things as they really are and feel and know deeply that we have no self at all. I will talk about this more in the full version of my book. For now, being aware of my thoughts, my conversations, and my actions was crucial because consciousness is the basis of deep meditation, which leads to Vipassana.

After I put myself together, my energy rose, and I began to make significant changes in the areas that had been problems in the past. I share those here in hopes that they may help you to see things you can do to improve your situation.

It starts with setting clear goals. I set goals for my theatre, my career, my health, and my love life. I asked "Why?" for every one of my goals. While I was working on each goal, I consciously chose to be in the moment and pursue it with passion, consistency, and focus, then analyze the results so I can do more of what is working and change the things that are not.

The key to making changes in your life is clarity of focus. That is what creating goals will do for you and by asking "Why is this important to me?" your inner motivation increases. Friedrich Nietzsche once said, "He who has a why to live for can bear almost any how."

As I got clarity on my goals, my results began to change. My theatre production got sponsors and a full house, and I earned a $30,000 profit. I decided to leave my high-paying TVC career to study more psychology and Buddhist teachings. I combined what I've learned with the acting that I love, and I share what I know without any expectations. When I tried this out on Facebook Live, my first broadcast had more than a million viewers and now I've become a full-time motivational speaker—a mindset trainer and a heartset speaking trainer.

I have two acting schools and own five successful companies. I've become a commentator for many TV shows in Thailand. I earn more than 10 times what I earned in the career that I once felt ashamed to get rid of. My health has improved as I now have fun on the treadmill by gaming with myself by practicing mindfulness with every step. I occupy my mind by saying left and right and watch my mind carefully when it flies to the future or the past. Then I bring it back to the present, to the left and right mind, speaking while walking. I've gotten physically and mentally fit and the time flies.

There are many ways to turn a task into an effortless flow. One of my students chooses to walk and watch his favorite TV series only on the treadmill so that he can anchor that fun feeling to the treadmill. The important part is to find your own way to have fun with your process.

Finally, in my love life, after I got clear on my goals, I decided to let my husband go, to free both him and me. I worked hard on raising my self-esteem by accepting every aspect of myself. Loving and compassionate me is the way I choose to see myself now no matter what. I learned to hug myself and my soul and forgive this little kid in me, to set myself free from guilt. After all, what I did in the past was the best I could do for my survival.

I started to see the good things in me that make me a good partner. And I thought deeply about what kind of man I want to walk with toward my goals. During those two years after the divorce, a few guys showed up, but I was not in a hurry because I loved myself enough to enjoy being with myself while I was waiting for the one I was looking for.

With this approach, sure enough, the right guy showed up. He cares for me and loves me, and I love him very tenderly. We have the same goals in life. We've been together for a happy 4 years now and he's been sitting opposite me in the house we've rented on our vacation in Germany, listening to my story, giving feedback, and now enjoying himself somewhere in the house while waiting for me to join him.

Today I don't consider myself a lucky woman because everything happens as I intend it, with passion, consistently working for my goals, focusing on them, and analyzing the results to continue making them better. Nowadays, I still enjoy asking myself how to make things better for those who are connected to me, while at the same time I really enjoy the present moment—sitting here typing this passage to tell you what I've learned with the hope this might help you in some way.

With my love and know that you are the best.

Rossukon Gonggate is a motivational speaker, TV judge, and acting coach who believes that inner peace can heal everything. She was born in her father's car on the way to the hospital in Bangkok, Thailand. She started her career as an acting coach and made her way to become the most successful acting coach/teacher in Thailand. She has changed the norm of Thai acting culture. One of the movies for which she provided coaching for the actors has become the highest grossing movie of all time in Thailand. Her coached actors have won many awards. Her acting school is very famous because most of the top actors in Southeast Asia have studied with her. She loves acting because it requires understanding human motivations and psychology, which are her passions. To deepen her understanding of these areas she has studied many different areas including Neuro Linguistic Programming, hypnotherapy, neuroscience, and Buddhism. She hosted her first Facebook Live on her page "Kru

Ngor Rossukon" and had over a million views within 5 days. She has become a mindset and heartset instructor/speaker and life coach for more than 200 organizations and has coached celebrities, politicians, athletes, and executives. She has been invited to be a TV judge on a TV program called Super10, which has had more than 20 million views and won the award as the best motivational TV program for two years running. These days she travels around Thailand to share her inner peace techniques with those who are disadvantaged, such as those in prison and schools in remote areas. You can download her free gifts from her Facebook page.

Chapter 4

TURNING YOUR CHALLENGES INTO MIRACLES

by Vivian Songe (Norway)

....

Yes, turning into a butterfly hurts. But what if your life's biggest challenges can make your creative life soar and potentially open up a whole new career for you?

As I stood in my backyard—mid-city, mid-winter—lighting a two-by-two-meter pile of men's clothing on fire, I popped the champagne. It made a muffled sound in the dark. Wearing only my best underwear, a black leather jacket, and long velour boots, I saw his red shirt—his favorite, only one week old—being devoured by the flames under the moon. I heard the fire crackle as it took a toll on his boxers in the snow, hoping that no one would report me to the police. I had never been this intensely open to all of my feelings: sad, angry, disappointed, disillusioned, enraged, and . . . strangely happy. I felt free.

Tapping Into Something Universal

Somehow, I knew that no matter how terrible, devastating, or life-altering the experience, I could always use it, refine it, push it out of my exact, personal experience and make it universal. As a writer, that's what you do. You can create an inner picture that is no longer specifically you, but universally everyone. Everyone who HAD stood in their backyard—mid-city, mid-winter—burning every piece of clothing their man owned to the ground. But also, everyone who hadn't, but wished they had, and now felt that in a way they had too, right there with me, freezing in their underwear, while they witnessed his turning into small orange tongues of light. They could live it with me, through me, this moment of disastrous victory of the heart. This is the magic of writing.

Have You Felt Someone's Story in Your Bones?

I bet you have felt this magic many times. I bet you have read at least one article or blog post or book that tells a true, enticing tale about someone else, and yet you felt the story in your bones as if it were YOUR story. Right?

Let me give you a rather famous example: *Eat Pray Love* by Elizabeth Gilbert. This woman's epic, life-altering journey in her all-time-high bestseller ended up as a Hollywood movie, starring Julia Roberts in the lead role. This is a book that just about every soul-searching woman on the face of this planet has devoured.

Why? Because Elizabeth's story burns. With honesty, adventure, introspection, truth-seeking, and love. And, not the least: with an authenticity that is felt through every page, through every word. Elizabeth decided to put the worst experience of her life into words and tell the tale of how she went through it—while traveling 3 continents—to begin to live a truthful life.

This is a prime example of the power that sharing your personal story can have. Yes, it is an art to convey it, but she is not the only one who has mastered it. Actually, you don't even have to be a professional writer to make an unforgettable impression.

Your unique story, when you practice your authentic way of telling of it, can make the whole difference.

What is Your Story?

Because this is the thing about the true tales that touch our soul: We can't get enough of them, can we? Maybe because they remind us of who we really are, deep down inside that tiny core, that nevertheless is connected to the whole universe. These stories show us our own grandness and connectedness.

Great authors often take something hugely human in their own life—devastating, shameful, life-altering or monumental—and write their way through it. They share it with the world, in their own unique voice, and gain enormous success because of it. Let me give you some more examples: Cheryl Strayed (*Wild*), Glennon Doyle (*Love Warrior* and *Untamed*), and Brené Brown (*The Gifts of Imperfection*).

Their lives as entrepreneurs, artists, speakers, and writers completely changed because they dared to dig deeply and expose something fascinating about their own life, and thereby a grain from all of our lives.

So, think about it for a minute: What do YOU want to share? What is your story, your message?

The Raw Truth

I knew that I would write when I was five years old. Like, really write. I figured that although everyone acted like the important things happened outside of our heads, bodies, and hearts, I could tell the real juice was on the inside, in our experiences, in everything between the lines. In the things that people were hiding from people, from their neighbors, from their spouses, from themselves. The truth was rawer between two covers. It was like it couldn't be touched by the politeness of all things, the greyish veil that we create to numb our experience of risk—of orange, of red, of fire.

So, I had to learn the magic of letters, right now, and make them mine. Maybe you know that feeling? The feeling of having something to tell, burning so brightly that you can see the whole creature inside of you—a yet unknown, glowing monster, searing the edges of your soul. But how do you write it, get it out into the world?

Any Detail Can Become a Story

This is what astonishes my writing students the most: That they can take any experience, detail, conversation, feeling, or thought from their very own lives and make it into something others crave to read. Something that will create the Meaning we all long for, and even make them the other M-word (M---y talks, after all). Because, yes, to truly live as a writer, you also need to live off of your writing, right? And it CAN be done.

Kine Nymo (38), a night nurse, had always been convinced that her writing was mediocre at best. A hobby, a cute little dream not to be reckoned with. Ever since her high school teacher told her that her writing was messy and unpredictable, she thought that's what it was. She thought there was no point in pursuing her dream about writing professionally, with a review like that. So, she stuck to her education and profession: nursing.

Kine Surprised Herself . . . and Everyone Else

Through my online course in freelance magazine writing, Kine realized that, no, her writing wasn't messy at all. It was intuitive, free, and open to new discoveries, like really good writing is. She discovered that she not only had a voice but that her voice was golden. It was filled with passion, curiosity, humor, and insight. Suddenly, thoughts, feelings, and words piled up, burning with desire to be let out, and when they finally did, they created magic.

Through those little snippets of genuine voice, she was able to begin her stories with something that the reader felt and identified with, something they enjoyed. An inner movie that they could picture and engage with. And when Kine used the building blocks she was given to create a professional article—the angle, the inverted pyramid, the framework, the values of interest—well, suddenly, she was invincible. She was a writer! Even though she only dared whisper it to the mirror in the morning, when everyone else was asleep.

Coffee With the Editor

The first article she wrote—ever!—was published in one of Norway's major women's magazines. Immediately afterward, the editor wanted to meet her and invited her for coffee. Kine landed 18 more assignments for that same magazine within the next 2 weeks, and within 3 months she could reduce her hours as a night nurse and spend more time with her 2 kids, her friends, her life. And she did. She did! She had tears in her eyes when she told me. Of disbelief, of gratitude, of happiness.

These are just a few of the stories Kine wrote right after my writing course that were featured in the national magazine before she could say "dream come true":

- "The Horrors of Mindfulness"
- "Are You Addicted to TV-shows?"
- "Just Like Your Mother"
- "Is Your Best Friend's Ex Off-Limits?"

From an Office Job to a Motorcycle Ride in the Desert

Ingrid Østang (38) worked at the Norwegian Directorate of Immigration and had never written articles before. She knew that there was something inside of her that wanted to break free, but she had no idea how to dig her way into that dark, unknown prison of her creative soul. Through my writing course, she removed stone by stone and got into the very core of her own artistic being. She blossomed like a daisy in spring and immediately sold 3 articles right after the course, to some of the most well-known newspapers and magazines in the country. Then she was invited by a celebrity to come to the desert in Morocco and write articles about him while he rode through it on a motorbike! Who would have known this was even a possibility? Ingrid was stunned.

Here are Some of Her First Printed Articles:

- "Break Free From Your Inner Critic"
- "Addicted to You. Are You Addicted to Others to Feel Valuable?"

- "Hooked on Kundalini Yoga"
- "Dreams Coming True in New York"

After succeeding in writing and selling numerous articles to different magazines, she took the next step in her personal artistic journey: She started writing songs. Now, she has released her first album and is due to go on tour around the country. She has also become a favorite freelance writer of one of the biggest and most respected newspaper magazines in Norway. Who would have thought?

Never Too Late

Merete Sillesen (63) started my freelance magazine writing course at the age of 59, an age when a lot of people have the impression that it is "too late." You can't possibly begin to pursue your dream this late in life, right? Wrong! Because in writing you can. All you need is a healthy brain and one hand that works.

Merete was a secretary and a childcare professional who wrote speeches for people on the side. When she learned the secrets behind the article formats and how to sell stories to a magazine, something fell into place inside of her, and she knew that this was what she wanted to do.

She has now published hundreds of articles in at least 28 different magazines and has since become one of the most popular journalists for human touch stories in Norway. She found her specialty and went for it, and she didn't let age or doubt hinder her. Now she is working full-time as a freelance journalist, being flown around Europe to interview people with exciting stories. But it started with her own. Isn't that just inspiring?

Here are Some of Her First Printed Stories:

- "New Friends at a Mature Age: We started talking, and have never stopped since!"
- "My Sister Got Dementia at the Age of 37"
- "Colorful Meditation. About the use of coloring books to find mindful peace."
- "What Should I Wear? Never Doubt Your Wardrobe Again."

What If You Were Enough?

None of these women thought it was possible. Not one bit! They didn't think they knew enough, felt enough, had enough, counted enough. But then they realized: I do know enough. In fact, I AM enough.

When presented with a clear method of how, what, and why, they were able to take any small detail from their lives and transform it from coal to diamond—make it desirable, readable, sellable. In short: Burning with that special magic that only a really good text can. And we all watch when something burns, don't we? We watch, but we don't always FEEL it, or allow ourselves to feel it. Not even when the burning is in our own chest, when something huge is seething in there, ready to get out.

Try These 6 Simple Exercises

Why not start out by doing these easy, fun, transformational exercises and see what shows up for you? They only take a few minutes, but they are very effective. I know this from my writing courses through several years, so I urge you to actually try.

Come play with your creativity and your inner glowing monster for a minute. It's fun, and who knows what it may lead to? What if, one day, that bestselling book on the newsstand is your own?

Take a few minutes, get out a pen and a piece of paper, and try it out:

1. Practice CREATIVE FLOW: Free writing without judgment

We are so used to making plans, to knowing everything before we start doing anything. Well, this is not how writing works. This is not how the soul works. In fact, this is not even how life works! When you enter a receptive state of mind and are completely open to whatever may show up, that is when FLOW hits you. The natural inherent creativity that we all can tap into at any time.

Keep a blank sheet of paper and a pen in front of you. Set a timer for 5, 10, or 15 minutes, and write uninterruptedly during that time. Don't stop to evaluate or judge. Just write whatever shows up. It is not important whether it is interesting or "good" or new. It can be "Oh my god, this is torture, I don't know what to write, and I shouldn't have left the door open, the wind makes my feet cold, I want a cup of coffee, but I really shouldn't have another one."

Do you know what happens when you let everything flow through you like this, without judgment? Then you become something grander than yourself. A portal, through which everything there is can flow through. Suddenly, when you have jotted down all of those seemingly insignificant thoughts, you have cleared the path for what lies underneath.

You see, we are all carriers of truths and profound messages, for ourselves and others, in our collective subconscious field. When you write and don't stop, the truths underneath all the junk will start to pour out. These are your golden treasures. Your gifts to yourself, and to the world. So, listen closely, and tell it like it is—for you.

2. Do as Walt Disney did: Practice POSITIVE SEGREGATION

I love Walt Disney. And it's not just because he created Donald Duck (okay, that too—who doesn't?) It's because of the way he is said to have organized the creative team in his business. It may very well be an urban myth, who knows, but it's still genius! Rumor has it that he not only gave his employees completely different tasks in the creative process. He also organized them on three separate floors of the building:

The Dreamers on top
The Realists in the middle
The Critics in the bottom

None of them should talk to each other or interfere with the other person's job. They should never be in the same room, not even on the same floor! Only when an idea was fully hatched by the Dreamers, it was sent on to the Realists, and then, later—when the time was right—to the Critics. They were to find weaknesses and check the quality, to make sure the ideas wouldn't fall apart. This way Disney ensured that the Dreamers were always completely free and uninterrupted so that they could create from an unlimited state of mind. Because we all too easily fall into the Critic's trap, don't we?

Well, no more of that, my friend. Practice positive segregation, in your mind! Never invite the Realist or the Critic to the party until the Dreamer has finished her job—imagining and fantasizing freely. Keep them on different floors of an imaginary building in your head. If the Realist or the Critic tries to sneak in the door to the Dreamer's floor, shut them out! Let them wait for their turn, like everyone else.

Some general rules for creativity

1. No rules
5. No criticism
3. No form
2. No expectations
4. No opinions

3. Who are you talking to? Identify your IDEAL READER

For each piece of writing, whether it is an article, a blog post, a book, or an Instagram post, pick someone specific to talk to, someone you know and cherish, so that you can speak directly to that person, in a language and style that reaches their heart. This makes everything you write much more relatable, authentic, and engaging. Because in spite of what people might think, you can't speak to everyone at once. Then no one will listen!

Just imagine how differently you would tell the exact same story to a child, your best friend, your mother-in-law, or your boss. Your tone of voice, what situations and details to include and exclude, what to highlight, and even the dramaturgy would change completely, right?

A good writer knows exactly who she is talking to, at any given time. By speaking directly to Jane, Tom, Laura, or Peter, you reach not only this exact person but everyone who is like them. In other words: By making your target narrow, you are making your hit percentage higher. If the target is wide, the "ammunition" will spread in all directions and land all over the place. The more particular, the harder you hit.

So why not talk to a good friend of yours, your brother, or someone you adore who represents the group you want to reach?

4. What is the main point? Identify THE ANGLE

In a nutshell, what is this particular text talking about? What is the ONE crystal clear message you want to convey? Jot it down in 1–3 sentences. Always imagine the reader asking you this question: "What's in it for me? Why should I read this piece? What is it going to give me? How will it change my life, if even just a little?"

Knowing what the main point is, the essence of each text, makes everything so much easier. Like choosing the title, the opening, and what to write in each subsection of the text. Keeping the angle—and the ideal reader—in mind, the order of things will more naturally fall into place. Try it out for yourself and see!

And remember: Always stick to your angle, throughout the whole text. If you write something great, and it doesn't fit with the angle, drop it and save it for another piece.

5. Make your text an ELEGANT WALTZ

For any text, always create 3 interconnected parts:

- **The hook in the beginning**. Start with something that will capture the reader's attention and make her head turn in your direction. "What? Are you serious? Did she really say/do that? What does she mean? That sounds interesting. Sounds like she's talking about me." Instant identification is important—something to immediately connect with the reader's emotions. The reader should see what you see and feel what you feel. Invite her into your story like in a movie, with an engaging scene that comes alive before her inner eyes. The use of real-life situations and original metaphors generally have this effect.

- **The juice/content in the middle.** This is where you give away the actual value, the content, the advice. The answer to "What's in it for me?" In short: What the reader is looking for. Always give away the content with credibility and an engaging voice, and don't forget the storytelling. Wherever you can tell a story or anecdote or insert a quote from someone you have talked to or interviewed, do that.
- **Pick up the loop in the end.** Make sure you end your text with something that is directly connected to the main point of the story and that goes elegantly together with the hook and the juice. So that the reader gets an experience of coherence. She should never be left with open ends or unanswered questions. Everything you have initiated should be completed.

And beware: The same goes for every subpart of the text! Under each subtitle, you should have the same principle in mind and create a coherent unity.

6. The "gimme more" factor: Let your GENUINE VOICE loose

We are speaking with our own, genuine voices every day, but somehow, when we are asked to put it on paper, it changes into a dry, bookish, greyly dressed version of itself, barely to be heard. It is astonishing how easily we forget our personalities as soon as we are going to write something!

Please, stop turning into a grey cupboard box. You don't need to. Be alive when you write. Give room for your flavor, your personality, your nuances, your gut feelings, your perspectives, your quirks—everything that makes you unique.

Ask yourself: How do you communicate and use words, naturally, among friends? How would YOU say that, if you didn't mimic anybody else? And how would you say it if you spoke, not wrote? Practice loosening up, being playful and natural. Be the *youest* you that you can be.

This is how you make people crave your words, your stories, your insights, your points of view. Rinse that throat and sing it! The song only you know, in the way only you know to sing it.

Dear reader, I wish you the best of luck in digging up your golden treasures. Please keep in touch. I can't wait to see your unique writing out there someday!

Vivian Songe *has been a freelance journalist and an editor for magazines and newspapers for nearly 20 years. She has an education in journalism, literature, film, social anthropology, languages, NLP, and EQ, and she uses them all to teach other people how to start living their writing dream. She has written hundreds of articles about lifestyle, psychology, travel, culture, literature, yoga, and health for at least 30 different magazines and newspapers. She has also co-written two books and worked as a media consultant for publishing houses. She is now working on her own books, fiction and nonfiction. She has founded her own online magazine journalism school, The Magazine Writer's Academy,* *where she teaches people how to get started writing professionally and earn a living from their writing. She also teaches creative writing and how to discover your unique voice. Her aim is to inspire and awaken the dormant writers of the world, who don't dare to believe in themselves or their message. Contact Vivian at* team@magazinewriters.academy. *This is your time!*

Chapter 5
OUT OF HIDING, INTO THE SUN
by Heidi Tuokila (Finland)

....

B lood spread on the black asphalt, turning it into a dark, red pool. An ambulance came with flashing lights and took him away. I was left alone in the inky black night thinking: It was all MY fault.

It was the night Princess Diana died. I heard it on the radio while the seemingly endless hours slowly turned into a new day. Earlier, I had managed to get to the hospital with the help of my friends. In panic, I explained he broke through a glass window. I told them I couldn't remember clearly what happened because I was so drunk . . .

But, of course, I remembered. I just had to wait for him to tell me what story we should tell. He told me we should say he fell and sharp stones cut his wrist. So the police would not be involved. And so I said what I was told, as, after all, it was all my fault. If only I would have said that I loved him, then this would not have happened.

During those moments of clarity when I knew I couldn't handle yet another fight, I'd walk away. But he always found a way to stop me. I turned to look back and there he was kicking at a big window as he vented his anger. I could see the danger and I ran to him begging him to stop. He stopped. And then suddenly, he hit the window with his hand and a shower of crystal-bright glass erupted.

He said we had to run. I thought we were running to avoid getting caught for breaking the window. Then I saw it. A stream of blood pouring out of his wrist. Two guys came over to help. Once he was taken away by the ambulance, I remember how empty and lost I felt on that beautiful, bright summer night in Lapland that suddenly felt like the pits of hell.

This is my story. The story of how I was able to transform my life with the hope it will help you transform yours. Have you ever wondered what happened in your life that resulted in this moment where you don't feel passionate about what you are doing any longer? And maybe, like me, you're having a hard time remembering how it feels to be totally happy and fulfilled. Whoever you are, wherever you are, and whatever has happened in your life, I invite you to join my journey. So that it can be our journey.

How It All Began

I looked at my older sister who was pretending to be a model walking on the catwalk in front of everyone. My little sister copied her and did whatever she could to be noticed. I quietly snuck out of the room and escaped from the "show." I took one of my many books and dived into a world of adventures. I heard the adults talking behind the door about me, saying how shy I was.

I was a perfect student getting top grades. I had a few great friends. I was really good at athletics and I loved it. But I only spoke in the classroom if I was asked to. I was happy but I felt there was something wrong with me as I had heard so many times that I was shy.

At the age of 15, I fell in love with a young man with a cute, wide smile and dimples. He was all over me, wanted to own me, and it made me feel so important and loved. He was old enough to go out to nightclubs and he loved getting really drunk.

At first, it was funny when he came back at night and did silly things that he couldn't remember in the morning. Sometimes it was a bit strange and also a bit scary that he needed me to tell him so many times that I really loved him and only him.

While I was busy being the perfect girlfriend, he started cheating on me. I was so hurt. While he was telling me how he could never live without me, that no one else would ever compare, he was cheating on me. And even though he was the one who was doing wrong, his anger grew.

I had never really learned to stand up for myself as I had always been so quiet. My already low self-confidence was becoming non-existent when he compared my body to beautiful curvy women in Playboy magazine. He would say: "How would you look without that nose?" "I could buy breast implants for you, but then all the other men would want you too." Yes, if I just would look better then there might be a chance that someone would someday love me.

I started comparing myself to every woman I met. Do you ever do that? I looked in the mirror with disgust, thinking: "You pathetic loser, such an ugly d**n thing." I would put makeup on, smile at my reflection, then hit my own face.

I started testing out my desirability with men big time. I needed men to tell me how amazing I was. I needed them to want me. In my head, I was so proud that I was getting back at my boyfriend. That I was hurting him too. Not that it was true. I was only hurting myself.

On bad days, I found relief by running as that was my biggest passion in life. I was on the Finnish Youth National Team and running 800 meters was my thing. When I was running, it was the only moment I ever had when I was not seeking love, approval, or appreciation. I just lived in that moment. You know how that feels, right?

A New Beginning

Have you noticed that there are signs everywhere? I got one sign in Thailand in 2018. I was having dinner with my friend and we were discussing relationships. She believed that you first have to find yourself before you can succeed in a relationship. This made me wonder if my relationship with my husband was a mistake, because I didn't know who I was when I first met him.

I started dating him straight after I broke up with my boyfriend and I was still an emotional mess at that time. I couldn't believe that someone could love me just as I was. I was for sure not ready for a new relationship, but I loved him with all of my heart.

Then I became pregnant and we got married. Life was so beautiful and full of love. Then I started getting sick. And for some reason, I never fully recovered before I was sick again. I lost my passion—my running. And, slowly, my beautiful puzzle started to unravel. I found relief through drinking and partying.

I was so lucky that I had my beautiful family, and I tried to rebuild the puzzle again and again. But it was so hard. Something had to change. So, I decided that I would be a successful businesswoman and I started a career in finance.

I believed that someday I could get back to running again. That day never came. Instead, I got sicker and more stressed from the work I was doing purely for the money. And I carried on this way for 11 years.

During all this time, on good days and bad days, my husband was there for me. And my beautiful daughter. Then along came a beautiful baby boy. Yet, there in Thailand, I was wondering if all the beauty in my life had been a mistake!

There was live music outside where I was eating dinner with my friend. And at that very moment when I had my doubts, the entertainer started playing our wedding song, Celine Dion's "When I Need You."

There was my sign. I believe that we're always in the place where we're supposed to be. Life doesn't happen *to* us. It happens *for* us. If we just keep our hearts open and notice, we will realize that there are no mistakes in life. The universe wants to lead us in the right direction.

My Transformation

After working in finance for a decade and suffering bad health for 15 years, I started searching. What was I searching for? I didn't know. But I knew I needed to find it.

I started studies to become a Holistic Skin Therapist while I was still working. There I was introduced to a book called *The Passion Test, The Effortless Path to Discovering Your Life Purpose* written by Janet Bray Attwood and Chris Attwood. Once I started following The Passion Test process, I started experiencing miracle after miracle. I was offered a golden handshake to leave my work and this made it possible for me to start my own business. I followed my intuition to participate in Janet's Passion Test Certification program, and it was the start of a total life transformation.

I also realized I had 5 big false beliefs about work and life. Let me share them. Maybe you can relate to them.

Changing Your False Beliefs

False Belief #1: You have to work hard in order to succeed . . .

Reality: This is true when I believe that thought. But if I believe that I can create financial freedom and success by following my passions then this becomes my truth. When I started following The Passion Test process, I realized that I can create my own ideal life. I set the intention that I can have an amazing work life and still have a lot of time for my family. After all, it is me who decides, right?

False Belief #2: I need people to see the potential in me in order to be successful . . .

Reality: Once I learned about self-love, I realized that I am the one who needs to see the potential in me. No one else. When I see my own potential, I don't need others to tell me that I have it. It is such a big relief to acknowledge your own potential and know that you will rock the world!

False Belief #3: It is a huge risk to leave your well-paid job to follow your dreams . . .

Reality: What I learned is that when you follow your passions, doors begin to open for you in a way that you would never have imagined. I had created a successful career by doing something that I didn't really like, so why would I not be able to do the same by focusing on what I love? I still felt a bit scared to jump into a totally new career path. But the truth is that it would have been even scarier to stay where I was: unhealthy and unhappy.

False Belief #4: If someone offers you a great job with great pay, take it . . .

Reality: Never make money-based decisions. I did. And in the end, it only led to stress and poor health. During all the years doing what I didn't love, I became more stressed, sick . . . and unhappy. I spent a lot of money on expensive clothes and fancy holidays in an attempt to feel sweet moments of pleasure and to convince myself that this was enough. Looking good on the surface didn't stop the suffering from within. Now I align my choices with my passions and use my heart and intuition.

False Belief #5: I need to focus on my weaknesses because when I fix them, I will be successful . . .

Reality: I don't need to be fixed. How is weakness even defined? I just have to stop comparing. And maybe I simply need to notice that I am doing the wrong kind of work. You will always feel the best when you can use your strengths and unique talents, do what you are good at, and do what you love.

How did my life change when I started my self-development journey?

I started to think: "What do I want to create in my life?" I looked at all the ingredients that had helped me to transform my life. Then I started cooking. I knew the dish I wanted to make. My dish was my company. I called it Holistic Health and Happiness with Passion. I carefully selected the main "SPICES" to flavor my dish. The SPICES that represent the core of my company and are, in my opinion, the key to holistic health and happiness are:

S—Self-Love
P—Passion
I—Intuition
C—Curiosity
E—Empowerment
S—Serenity

Each word holds a key for you to unlock your miraculous life.

S—Self-Love: I make the best possible choices for myself. I am true to myself and have the courage to say what I want from life. I take care of myself as I am valuable. Janet Bray Attwood has the most powerful course called "Mastery of Self-Love," which touched the core values of my being and changed my life forever for the better. Through loving myself fully, I can radiate love to others around me.

P—Passion: I follow The Passion Test process and do it regularly to stay aligned with my passions and to create clarity in my life. I learned and began to practice the secret that guarantees a passionate life: "Whenever you're faced with a choice, a decision, or an opportunity, choose in favor of your passions."

I—Intuition: "The intuitive mind is a sacred gift and the rational mind is a faithful servant. We have created a society that honors the servant and has forgotten the gift." ~ Albert Einstein.

I have intuition in my toolbox for life. I trust it when I make decisions. When I started trusting my intuition, it started speaking even more loudly.

C—Curiosity: When I had my second child, I looked for a photo album of my childhood to check if I was once like him: full of curiosity and joy. I found my answer from the pictures where a little girl with a fringe was glowing with happiness and had a smile up to her ears.

What happened to that girl? I realized that the two biggest events that caused me to lose my curiosity were the unhealthy relationship with my ex-boyfriend and losing my biggest passion, running, because of my health.

But if you have once had something and lost it, doesn't it also mean you can get it back? I was in a networking meeting and shared with others that not long ago I was a quiet introvert and they couldn't believe what they were hearing. One woman said "No way, not you. Do you know what you are? You are curious and I love that about you." I had gotten it back! We can all find it in ourselves as we were born that way.

E—Empowerment: Sharing what you believe is the best way to manifest it in your own life. When Janet Bray Attwood interviewed great masters, they all said the same thing: "The secret of being happy is in giving." When you help others and give to others, you will experience deep joy in your life.

S—Serenity: I love this word. It is defined in the dictionary as "the state of being calm, peaceful, and untroubled." This is what I want my life to be. I achieved serenity in my life by focusing on holistic health—my mind, body, and spirit.

I wish I would have joined self-development courses much earlier in my life but back then I failed to see the value in them. I didn't see them as investments or how they could benefit me. To make it easier for you to decide whether self-development courses could benefit you, I invite you to take the following SPICES test.

EXERCISE: How SPICY is your life?

Go through each word and think about how true it is in your life. Write a few clear sentences to describe how can you see this aspect in your life:

S—Self-Love:
1. I make the best decisions for me when . . .
2. I am proud of myself because . . .
3. When I look in the mirror, I see . . .

P—Passion:
1. When I wake up in the morning, I am excited because . . .
2. I feel full of passion and joy at work when I . . .
3. I am clear about my top 5 passions in life, which are . . .

I—Intuition:
1. The last decision I made based on my intuition was . . .
2. When I look at my past, I can see that my intuition helped me when . . .
3. When I have decided to do something, but my gut feeling says no, I . . .

C—Curiosity:

1. The last time I tried something new was . . .
2. When someone asks me to try something new, I feel . . .
3. I find my inner child when I . . .

E—Empowerment:

1. I used my unique gifts to help my friend with . . .
2. Other people often thank me for . . .
3. I am surrounded by like-minded friends and family when . . .

S—Serenity:

1. I feel at peace when . . .
2. I feel my life is effortless because . . .
3. When I go to sleep, I am grateful for . . .

I developed the simple SPICES test to check in with myself on how well I am doing in my life. I realized the importance of doing this after I saw myself still slipping back into unhealthy habits. It is easy to get too excited with one area of life, like work, but then lose your attention on other areas like exercising.

What did you learn about yourself? Was it easy to come up with examples? If it was, congratulations! Your life has great flavor in it! But if it wasn't, don't worry. Just notice where you were struggling and think about why that is. Maybe it's not an area where you have been focusing. Could it be an area that would make a difference in your life if it would grow?

I never thought my life could change this much in just a few years. I am helping people all over the world to become masters of their own lives. I love spreading the message of following one's passions, growing in self-love, and living a life of holistic health. This is my path. What is yours? If you need help to find out or any support along the way, know that you are welcome here.

***Heidi Tuokila** left her finance career and transformed her life. She was sick for 15 years but fought her way back to holistic health and happiness. She is the founder of a company called I'm with U by heidimirella, Holistic Health & Happiness with Passion. She is a Master Trainer and Director of The Passion Test Programs in the Nordic Countries. During the last few years, she has traveled all over the world to assist and to be a trainer at Passion Test Certification and Master Trainer courses. She is also a holistic skin and beauty therapist, healer, and spiritualist. Heidi can be reached at* heidi@byheidimirella.com.

Chapter 6
FINDING THE WAY HOME

By Miki Ikatura (Japan)

· ·

I t was late at night. I heard a knock on the door of OHANA house. I opened the door and was greeted by a young mother, standing on my doorstep, holding her two-month-old baby with her three-year-old daughter standing beside her.

I quickly told them to come in, got her some tea and something to eat, then she told me her story. "I can't stop abusing my daughter. I'm terrified that I'll kill her, and I can't bear it. I hate myself!" She told me how she had been abused as a child and all her rage seemed to come out around her little three-year-old. I told her she needed to rest, and she told me, "I've wanted to cry for so long." And then she did, sobbing in my arms as she opened up about her pain.

69

She stayed at the OHANA House to rest her heart and body. Eventually, she began to value and love herself. She learned to cook for her kids and has not raised her hand to her daughter since.

This is just one of many stories we encounter at the OHANA project. These are the forgotten and discarded in our society.

I myself have been the victim of abuse and violence for more than 40 years. Such problems usually have a common root cause: lack of love.

Mother Teresa said, "My weapon is love."

In my own life, I have searched and yearned for that "love." Now I share the same message too. "My weapon is love. Love is all I've got."

The greatest discovery of life is that the universe is love itself.

Love is the source of life, and its influence can change the desire to die to the will to live. It can transform sadness into kindness. It can convert pain into strength. Love cannot be lost, and love is always enough; it is infinite. Love has infinite power to create change and transform things in a way beyond our human imagination. Love has the power to crystallize miracles.

After many years of tending to the silent cry for help of children who have been abused, there is one thing that I know for certain: The children who have been hurt are the heroes who will save this earth.

"Help me!"

These children cried out from a very young age.

To just be loved.

To be held.

That's all.

Yet these children lived every day in a reality where there was no one to answer their call, to listen to their pleas. The hand they hoped would love and hold them would instead punch and hit them and shower them with abuse.

There is something that happens to children who experience this. At a certain point, they numb their feelings to not feel any emotion at all. They close their hearts and stop trusting people. The experience of living through such unimaginable things infects their hearts and bodies and becomes a dark, deep wound.

In the island country of my Japan, one after the other, many children are killed through abuse.

"Help me."

Their continuous cry for help disappears one by one. We cannot have a society like this. We cannot build a country upon crying children. We cannot build a country upon murdered children.

While Japan is the third largest economy in the world, surprisingly, one in every seven children lives under the poverty line.

At the age of 12, I became a street child. When I was 14, I was put in a foster home. But at that facility, I was punched and kicked every day. I was told, "You're less than a piece of rotten trash thrown away by your parents."

Being physically and verbally abused repeatedly, I didn't think I was worthy of living. I had no shred of self-respect or self-esteem left. All day, every day, I only thought about dying. I was devastated by life.

"When I grow up, I want to help kids like me."

This heartfelt desire kept me surviving every day. When I made this vow to myself at 14, I think I wanted to be saved more than anyone. If there was even one person who helped me, who loved me, I wouldn't have wanted to die at all. I believed that adults had taken control of my life and I hated them all.

"I don't want to become an adult."

I didn't think there was anyone I could trust in this whole world.

My heart was heavy and hardened as if it had a cold, heavy, metal, shutter door over it and it would never open. Over many months and years, I put a lid on my feelings and numbed myself so I wouldn't feel at all.

The 20 years I lived believing that I was a no-good human being felt like hell. I blamed everyone else for my own inability to love myself or to love anyone else. I had no idea why I didn't know how to receive love.

When I finally gave myself the same love I was pouring into children and others, I realized how much I didn't love myself. I never accepted my life and spent my time looking away, running away. Who was I running from? From myself.

Have you ever felt like that? If so, then this chapter is for you.

It's natural to feel like running away when the pain is so intense. But that's not where you find freedom. No matter how much I ran away, I always discovered that I was still there. Eventually, I had to face myself. I consciously decided to love myself through the pain and the deep wounds of my abuse.

To jumpstart my emotions, I had to first melt my frozen heart with passion, so I asked the universe to provide me with a passionate, emotional master. And, lo and behold, an amazing, passionate woman appeared in my life. Her name is Janet Bray Attwood.

Janet treated me as if I was her family. And she said to me, "The seminar for you is self-love. Our hearts are the same. Come and take the self-love seminar. It's going to be held for the first time in Denmark. You must come, especially after having your soul so wounded."

So, I went to Denmark, to face myself and to finally get to the Pandora's box that was hidden deep down in my heart.

With courage, and with love, I released my fears. I stopped trying to please others by trying to guess what they might think of me. I stopped holding back my emotions and instead I decided to be honest and true to my feelings, honoring my intuition, and I began to turn my life around.

This was completely the opposite of the way that I had been living until then.

Now that I could hear my own voice, I could hear the voices of the children. I could hear so many of them asking for help. From refusing to go to school, to domestic violence and abuse, to complicated relationships with people at home and work, to divorce. I found children and adults suffering . . . alone, struggling to live. I decided that I would hear their silent cries and hold them with love.

In 2016, I began the OHANA kids' eatery where children and single mothers can eat for free as one of my OHANA projects. "Ohana" means "family" in the Hawaiian language. From babies to the elderly, every week about 70 people gather to eat together with complete strangers, and we have continuously created a space where people create a family bond beyond their blood relatives. More and more children come to ask if there's anything they can do to help.

But I also had a dream of creating a family home where people of all generations—from babies to the elderly—could gather.

In 2017, when I returned from my time with Janet in Denmark, I found the ideal place and opened the House of Ohana in Gosen City, Niigata. The House of Ohana is a place for young people who have to leave the foster care system at age 18 and for people who have been hurt by abuse and domestic violence. It is also a place where the elderly can go and be surrounded by people of all generations instead of spending time alone.

I've learned that when you don't have a family home or anyone you can rely on, it's easy to fall into the search for instant gratification and/or to run after quick money, which could lead you to the dark side of life. However, if you have a family and a home you can go back to, it can be a light of hope during your suffering and struggles.

At the same time, I have continued to respond to emergency calls of help (like those at the beginning of this chapter) from people through our OHANA SOS rescue.

Mother Teresa also said this: "Be careful of your habits; for your habits become your character. Be careful of your character, for your character becomes your destiny."

If the habit of being starved for love warps your character and ruins your sense of destiny, then you can change your destiny by repeating a fulfilling, loving habit and change your character to eliminate the negative self-talk and self-destructive behavior that comes from abuse.

For 16 years, I have lived with a deep wound every day. I faced the children and tended to their hearts and bodies to give them love.

Not understanding love. Not loving myself. Now that has changed.

As a result, I've learned some fundamental lessons that can help you create loving habits in your own life and the lives of your children.

1. Live honestly and live out loud

Voice your honest truth. Use your voice to ask for help when in need, and honestly communicate your feelings. Be brave and ask for what you want.

2. Choose love

Love is the foundation and basis of all there is in this world. We create our own worries and fears, and if you choose to act from love, love will always return to you.

3. Don't be bound by "normal"

There is no need to deny, criticize, or judge. That will only stop you from taking action. Do not be afraid of other people's reactions.

4. Be present in this moment, right here

Act as you feel, and do not think of the "why not" to act that way. Just imagine how you can crystallize joy now, in this moment.

5. Believe in yourself

No matter what sort of experience, your experience is your fortune. There is always a lesson in it. Choose to see everything as being what's best for you. When you do this, you'll discover that every experience contributes to helping you become more fully you.

6. Be happy within yourself

The energy of happiness is the vibration of love. Be grateful to have this life. Balance and harmonize the part of life in which you live depending on yourself with the part of life in which you lean on others for support. That will give you happiness.

There is something I tell everyone that I work with.

Please be happy within yourself first before you try to help others. Children will understand most when you are full of love and have the freedom to feel. So please, be happy within yourself first.

Children who cannot receive love and continuously hurt themselves more and more need to be held and wrapped up in love until they can receive that love and find their resilience and strength. There is no other way than love to heal something that was hurt by the absence of love.

The power of love is endless and infinite, and it comes with the definite certainty that you will always be provided with what you need.

As I gave love and held these precious, deeply hurt children, I began to realize that this is my life's purpose.

When you open yourself to start giving yourself love, then you will begin to discover your own life's purpose. It starts with clarifying what the things are you love and care about most in life—your passions. Then, as you make choices every day in favor of those passions, you'll discover that your life begins to feel more and more full of meaning. Doing that requires loving yourself.

To love the person in front of you is to love yourself. If you don't love yourself, you cannot love the person in front of you. What I can do for these children is help them regain their self-esteem and love themselves. If I love myself fully, no matter what kind of child is in front of me, I am able to show them the importance of loving yourself. And I can show them how to get their emotions flowing again.

Children who have had their hearts and bodies hurt . . . mothers who blame and hate themselves . . . the negative chain reaction of abuse can only be severed with love. All I have is love.

In the beginning, I worked alone in tending to these mothers and children, but now I have so many people all over Japan who help and support me with love.

Up until now, Japanese society has always placed more value on one's academic background than one's individual character. But this is about to change, and the age of honoring each person's individuality is arriving. And your own individuality is expressed through your own passions—from connecting with and choosing in favor of the things that really matter to you. That's why the House of OHANA has been such a blessing for me.

Kids who know what they like and don't do the things they don't want to do, who are not good in groups, and who struggle at school are actually at the forefront of this next era.

By clarifying what you love and giving that to others . . . your greatest abilities will become your work. This means that we will no longer work just for money but to bring joy to someone else by our own actions. Work will become activities that fill our souls with joy. The chain reaction of love begins here.

I opened up the OHANA Academy to teach children how to love themselves. The academy is for children who choose not to go to school, to lead their own lives and decide what they want to express. It is for those who don't want to be used by others but to become a leader in Japan where people can live doing what they love. It's an academy that children run for themselves, so they can believe in themselves as leaders.

The OHANA academy brings out the infinite possibilities, willpower, and love within children. And I hope to raise children who are able to design their own lives as they love themselves so that they will lead us to a brand-new age.

"Remembering how to be loved by loving."

"Remembering how to love by being loved."

All I can do is love and keep giving love.

We are not alone. We are here to help each other and support each other to create a world where our dreams come true.

Please support these children who are choosing to live in this moment, who choose to let go of what's "normal" or "correct" to live freely by their own values.

This planet is a planet of love, and that's why love is what creates endless miracles. Love is the source of everything, and love is our moving force.

Why? Because we were born in love. Let love be your own path to freedom.

*At age 12, **Miki Ikatura** ran away from home and became a street child. At the age of 14, she was sent to a public children's independence support institution. At 16, she gave birth to her first daughter. At 19, divorced and now a single mother, she lived in a park with her child. In 2004, based on her own experience, she started rescuing and supporting those with the trauma of abuse/domestic violence; physical and mental scars; developmental disorders, withdrawal, suicide and similar challenges. She called it OHANA Life Rescue. In 2011, Miki founded the non-profit organization, "Over-genes," committed to strengthening the bonds between mother and child. In 2018, she launched a shared house called OHANA house in Niigata, Japan to shelter children and mothers in emergencies. Now there are three OHANA houses in Niigata, Fukushima and Okinawa. She also operates a weekly OHANA Diner there to serve free meals for kids, single mothers/fathers and lonely old people in need. In 2019, she formed the Foundation for Social Contribution Support (FESCO) and was honored as a social contributor.*

Chapter 7
WHEN WORK IS MISERY . . .
FINDING THE WAY OUT

By Toyokazu Tsuruta (Japan)

. . . .

I'd been lying to myself for many years. On top of that, I cheated many customers out of what they could have had while I was at Microsoft.

It may not have been noticed by others, but my heart felt paralyzed.

Over my years at Microsoft as a recruiter, I did thousands of interviews, saw lots of careers get created, and saw others come apart. A lot of the time I was frustrated.

I'd think, "This candidate will be recruited if they just change this part of their application slightly." Or I'd think, "This candidate's style is more likely to appeal to that manager." Even though I had these thoughts, and I knew I could help these candidates, the rules didn't allow me to coach applicants, so I felt that my hands were tied.

For a long time, I kept thinking that I could help these applicants so much more directly. So, finally, I left Microsoft and became a career consultant. In this role, I could guide candidates, help them understand how to present themselves so they'd get hired.

While I enjoyed consulting with clients on their careers, most of the workload required of me made me miserable. I offered candidates many services: website creation/maintenance, accounting, shooting and editing videos, writing blog articles, and much more. Very little of it was what I really enjoyed doing, but I thought, "This is what I have to do to support myself."

It was a great contradiction. The whole idea of going out on my own was to have the freedom to do what I enjoyed. Yet I wasn't enjoying any of it!

On top of that, my income as a career consultant wasn't very good and didn't seem to be getting better. I was just lying to myself about having freedom. My heart was paralyzed, stuck in work I abhorred, and my sales didn't rise, no matter what I did.

I felt sorry for myself, but I didn't know what to do or which way to turn. I felt very emotional. It was not a fun time.

So, I looked for other work that makes more money. I allied my company with an internet marketing company and through various trial and error experiments, finally, sales began to pick up. Finally, my business was on track.

Then one day, I was eating a traditional Japanese food called yakisoba. I'd eaten yakisoba many times before, but this time the taste was unusual. In fact, I couldn't taste it at all. I asked my wife what was wrong with the food that it had no taste. Surprised, she said it had the same taste it always does. But I couldn't taste anything!

Then I noticed that I could hardly move the right side of my face. I couldn't close my mouth completely. When I'd try to take a drink, the water would run out of the right side of my mouth.

My right eye was closed, and I couldn't open it. I was frightened and this paralysis didn't go away. So, finally, I went to the hospital where I was diagnosed with facial nerve paralysis and was hospitalized for two weeks. I was given an intravenous steroid drip and physical therapy. As a result, I completely recovered, but during this time in the hospital, I had lots of time to reflect.

I asked myself, "Why did this happen?"

Even when I asked the doctor, he couldn't tell me the cause. Even without anyone telling me the cause of this sudden malady, I felt strongly that something wasn't right in my life.

"The way I'm living my life is wrong. Maybe it's because of stress and I need to do something."

Even though my business was now doing well, I was doing work that was not a good fit for me, so stress kept accumulating day after day.

I had thought that as an entrepreneur I would have freedom. But it didn't work out that way and, instead, I was worse off than ever. Now I was just working for money. It became all about vanity—looking good to others—while at the same time my heart was in pain.

I tried many therapies in my attempt to manage the situation and sometimes they would help a little, but eventually, I felt myself drifting downhill again.

Then one day I thought, "Is passion what I'm missing? If I can live passionately, then I'm sure my life will change!" This thought was so strong that I searched the internet for the word "passion."

The first results were not helpful. They were about romantic relationships between men and women. This wasn't what I was looking for. I tried searching for "how to live more passionately," but no results came up in Japanese.

So, finally, I did a search for the English word "passion." I looked for who would be the best in the field of passion, and I found a book called *The Passion Test* on the U.S. Amazon website. I got the book and tried out the process described in the book with my friends. It was great. It became very easy to clarify what I was passionate about. I was amazed!

I went online and found that Janet Bray Attwood, co-author of *The Passion Test*, was offering a training course in Vancouver, Canada. I signed up and flew from Japan to Vancouver to take this 4-day passion training with Janet.

As the course progressed, there was an opportunity to demonstrate what we were learning in front of everyone. Janet likes to create surprises, so she said the ones who don't raise their hands will be chosen. At that moment, I didn't raise my hand and, sure enough, I was chosen.

I stood in front of the whole course, feeling both excited and anxious since my English was not that good. But, surprisingly, once I started presenting, I really enjoyed it and the reaction of the course participants was very positive. Janet said, "You are amazing! You look like Tony Robbins when you present." Since I felt Tony Robbins was the world's top lecturer at that time, this was a huge compliment.

Janet told me, "Something is different about you when you speak in front of a group. You have a natural talent for public speaking." Before that, I had thought that I would never be able to speak in public. I didn't think I could do it, so I told myself that I didn't want to do it.

But when Janet told me that I was a good speaker, I started to feel that maybe I could do it. A desire began to grow in me to publish my own book and to become a successful speaker.

It turned out that I was the first person from Japan to take the Passion Test Certification course. At the end of the course, I was so excited that I told Janet, "I want to bring you to Japan and get *The Passion Test* published in Japanese." Janet was a little reluctant. Apparently, others had told her they wanted to translate *The Passion Test* into their language, and nothing had come of it.

Still, somehow, I believed that I could do it. I guess my passion was on fire.

When I returned to Japan, I thought about how to translate this book and get it published. Janet didn't think I could do it, but I was really determined. I had no idea how to create a book proposal, so I bought two books to figure it out. I tried to write a query letter, but I wasn't sure how to write a project plan for this book.

Then I heard about a publishing camp being offered by a bestselling author in Japan. The advertising said, "I will tell you how to succeed in publishing and answer all the questions you have about translating a foreign book for publication." So immediately I joined that training course, and I learned what is required to publish a book and create a successful book proposal.

Surprisingly, at the evening meal, the course instructor happened to sit right in front of me. We talked and he encouraged me. Then I said to myself, "I can sell this book." The feeling that I could do this became very strong.

The only problem was, I am not a professional translator. But then Janet put me in touch with a translator named Yoko Yuile whom she'd met at an event. When I contacted Ms. Yuile, she responded very positively. It turned out that she liked *The Passion Test* and had wanted to work on translating it for some time.

The next challenge was that I had no direct connection with any Japanese publisher. But, by chance, a business partner had a connection to Forest Publishing, which was a well-known publisher that was in touch with the trends. They liked the idea of publishing *The Passion Test* if Janet would come to Japan to help promote the book. And since I now had a professional translator to help translate the book, all other objections were gone.

Within a year, the book was released with a new, Japanese title: *Do It Only For Your Heart!* Thanks to its many readers, *The Passion Test* spread widely in Japan. I started giving Passion Test workshops and created a career as a speaker. During this time, I was working on own book, *The Book Without "Mendokusai"*.

"Mendokusai" is a word used daily in Japan. It refers to different things in different contexts, but in general means something that's a hassle, bothersome, a pain to deal with. So, my book can be thought of as "how to have a life without hassles."

Apparently, it struck a chord with many people. It ended up selling over 170,000 copies and my dream had finally come true.

1. What I hope you will notice is that my dream came true through the power of my passion and through using the power of others. Here was the process:

2. I wanted to discover my passions and how to live a passionate life. So, I went to Canada and took the Passion Test Certification course.

3. The course was so valuable for me that I had a deep desire (passion) to see it translated and published in Japanese.

4. With no publishing experience, no translation experience, no knowledge of the "how" to see my desire fulfilled, the people and the things needed in order to make it happen were drawn to me—I got some books; I learned of a course that taught how to publish a book; Janet introduced me to Yoko Yuile, a professional translator; my colleague introduced me to Forest Publishing; Janet was willing and open; and so my passion came to be and *The Passion Test* was published in Japan.

5. With the experience I gained from working on *The Passion Test*, I made contacts and learned how to publish my own book.

Choosing a topic that was very dear to me, I was able to create a book that became very popular.

Could I have planned this sequence of events in advance? Absolutely not! But by consistently following my passions and then making use of the knowledge, experience, and power of others, I was able to create a bestselling book and to create the kind of life I had always dreamed about.

You see, even if you have a dream that seems impossible, it can be possible when you make use of the power of others. In order to make use of that power, the key is passion. Passion gives you the courage to make requests of others and the excitement and energy you radiate when you're passionate about something are attractive to others. They want to say yes to you.

Today, I write and lecture as an author. When I was a consultant, I tried to do everything myself. As a result, I ended up doing many things that I didn't enjoy. When you do that, you end up unhappy and miserable. No one wants to be around that kind of energy.

The key to removing the misery in work is to focus on the things you love to do, the things that you're good at doing, and leave the other work to others. I love writing and speaking about the things I'm passionate about, so that's what I do now and leave the other things to others. Things like customer acquisition, marketing, sales, customer support, website creation, video shooting, and editing . . . I leave these things to my producers and collaborators.

If you are unhappy in your work, here are your two keys: passion and using the power of others. When you focus on the things you love and the things you're good at, then use others' skills and talents for the things you don't enjoy, you'll discover that not only do you enjoy your work, but the results are greater as well.

Toyokazu Tsuruta is a bestselling author in Japan. More than 200,000 people have bought his books. As a behavioral psychology consultant, he has supported life transformation for more than 10,000 people, leading them to their true calling and helping them to achieve their dreams. Before starting his own company, Toyokazu worked in human relations at Microsoft. His experiences interviewing thousands of people provided him with a vast knowledge about various career paths. His achievements at Microsoft placed him in the top three percent of his peers. Because of his successes, he was awarded an Asia Gold Club Award. Janet Bray Attwood, New York Times bestselling author and creator of The Passion Test, *credits Toyokazu for single-handedly bringing* The Passion Test *to Japan. As a result, there are now over 200 Passion Test facilitators in Japan and tens of thousands of people have completed this simple process for discovering one's passions and living a passionate life.*

Chapter 8
FROM EXISTING TO THRIVING

by Julia Tseng (Taiwan)

....

"Just be sure to notice the collateral beauty. It's your profound connection to everything."
       —from the movie Collateral Beauty

I t is said, men have two births; one is the birth of the body, and the other is the awakening of the soul. After recovering from the lowest point of my life, I feel like I have been given a second life. Without the turning point, I would not appreciate the beauty within everything, everyone, and every moment. I would not feel so much love around me. I would not know how to love others.

My life has become a blessing. In this chapter, I'll share with you how that happened, what the keys were to that transformation, so you can apply them in your own life.

My Lowest Point

2007 was a very important year. On January 9, 2007, Steve Jobs announced a revolutionary new product to the world, the first iPhone. Ever since that time, the iPhone and the copycat phones it inspired have completely changed every human being's daily life. Many people cannot survive a day without carrying their smartphone with them.

Among the lives that were changed by this announcement were the employees who worked for Nokia, Moto, and Blackberry. I wish I could say that I foresaw this change and that's why on January 2, 2007, I chose to join one of the smartphone pioneer companies, HTC. I'd like to be able to say that my life took off with the rising success of the smartphone industry and now I am enjoying the comfortable retirement life everyone envies.

In fact, the reality was exactly the opposite. Collaborating with Android, HTC had explosive growth from 2007 to 2012, while I fell flat on my face. I had sunk into an abyss of darkness.

If you met me during 2007–2012, this would be my introduction: "Hello, my name is Julia. My favorite food is hamburger, and the drink I love the most is anything with alcohol." Like the billionaire villain Richmond Valentine in the movie *Kingsman: The Secret Service*, I loved to eat a hamburger with red wine. Of course, my drink was not a 1945 Chateau Lafite Rothschild, but I was not kidding. If there was a camera following me, like on *The Truman Show*, this was my life:

10:15 a.m., Weekly Meeting

I present my project status with dark circles under my eyes. I stayed up late to prepare the summary, hoping to get Boss "Z's" instruction to go for Proposal A or B. Boss "Z" didn't pay attention to what I was saying. "Z" turned his head to my supervisor "Y" and said, "I don't understand what she is talking about. After this meeting, you and related staff come to my office and then we'll make the decision."

12:15 p.m., After Meeting

After the meeting, my supervisor "Y" reports to Boss "Z" with the exact same summary report I presented earlier this morning. "Y" gets "Z's" approval 5 minutes after he enters "Z's" office. I was not qualified to enter "Z's" office, so I waited outside, heard "Y" say exactly the same things I had said earlier. I feel frustrated and hurt . . .

12:30 p.m., Lunch

An endless litany of mocking, complaints, hate, and frustration. Lunch is a smorgasbord of negativity among my colleagues and me.

2:33 p.m., Issue Review Meeting with Design Team—A

I yell with anger, "Did you bring your brain to work? Didn't we just discuss this? Aren't you here? Why are you asking me the same thing again now?"

3:44 p.m., Issue Review Meeting with Design Team—B

I yell with a mocking voice, "You are logically inconsistent. Do you really know what you're talking about? Is this report fabricated? Why is it different from the data I just heard?"

4:22 p.m., Issue Review Meeting with Testing Team

I am impatient, absent-mindedly continuing to review the endless issues list with various departments, discuss, and list the action items of each issue.

5:43 p.m., Production Review Meeting

I yell with rage, "You said, this is not your business. He and he said this is not their business either. No one wants to take responsibility. Okay, fine, let's quit together and we all don't need to do anything anymore." I, the meeting host, walk out and leave a group of astonished colleagues in the meeting room . . .

7:30 p.m.

I sit at my cubicle, eating dinner, summarizing meeting minutes of the day, and replying to emails at the same time.

9:45 p.m.

As is my routine, I visit different labs at the company before the end of the day, to check if there are any new updates and to discuss the action plan if we got any surprises or unexpected testing results.

11:23 p.m.

I park the car, walk across the street to the 7-11 opposite my apartment, buy some snacks (potato chips most of the time) and alcohol, then go back to my 1-bedroom suite. As soon as I enter my apartment, I take off the suit, wipe the makeup off my face, sit on the floor with my back against the bed, pour myself a glass of wine, drink up, top off another glass, take a fistful of potato chips, put them into my mouth, grab the TV remote control, and turn on the TV. I stare at the TV, but don't really "watch" it. One moment I am laughing at the ridiculousness of it all. The next moment I am weeping at the hopelessness of it all. Later I shake my fist in the air. There are lots of voices, lots of emotions in my head, replaying all kinds of fragmented images from the day. I replay the annoying moments, the shouting, being humiliated, being misunderstood. Over and over they play in my head like bad TV reruns.

1:30 a.m.

The alcohol worked; my mind slows down; I curl up and fall asleep on the floor . . .

3:44 a.m.

I've sobered up. Now, there are three possible phenomena:

First, my whole body is trembling, unable to move, beset with all the fears in my head.

Second, without any reason, I start crying. Tears fall like a leaky faucet, unstoppable.

Third, I crawl into bed. I'm so afraid to face the arrival of tomorrow. I can't fall asleep again. I begin to imagine all the different ways I can commit suicide . . .

5:15 a.m.

As the sky turns fish-belly white in the east, I am so exhausted, I finally fall asleep for a while.

8:00 a.m.

I get up, freshen up, put on my mask, and get ready for work.

Working under high pressure and long hours made me lose my patience. I had long forgotten how to respect others and myself. I was living two different kinds of lives. During the day, I put on my mask and armed myself to lead the project. At night, I lived in a deep, dark abyss.

As a result, as you can imagine, I messed up my project. I went from hero to pariah. Once I completely gave up, I drank more, I had more time to complain because I didn't have to work overtime every day. I plunged into a cesspool of negativity.

I heard my soul screaming, and I died inside.

Letting Go

Our scene switches to London during my vacation time later that year. It was a perfect sunny day in June, about 5:30 in the evening. I was dressed casually, a pink sweater and jeans, ordering a cup of Guinness at the Market Porter Pub. Around me was a crowd of people in suits, seemingly just off work. They stood outside the pub, cheerfully chatting in 3s or 4s. I brought my Guinness to the other side of the street, sat down on the roadside, and drank up the joyous scene.

At that moment, I suddenly realized I missed happy faces very much. I couldn't help wonder and ask myself, "When was the last time I sincerely smiled or laughed? When was the last time I sat down, talked to, and cared about my family and friends?" I shook my head, gulped down my Guinness, and thought, "These years, I kept chasing after endless tasks at work, day in and day out. No personal life. This is not right." Then, I looked up, saw the beautiful, sunny day, and decided to take a walk with a smile this evening.

But I only smiled for 10 minutes. Then I started to cry. I cried because I was happy and touched by what I had felt and seen. "What a wonderful world. Isn't it great to be alive because I can bathe in the sun, I can sing, I can smile, I can travel, I can see so many beautiful people? Why the hell have I locked myself in a dark corner for so many years?"

That day, I promised myself: "There must be places on Earth that are not ruled by an iron fist. I don't believe there is no place for a happy me on this planet. I want to earn my life back. I want to change. I want a bright, happy, and fulfilled life."

After that trip, work was no longer the first priority in my life. It no longer occupied most of my time and attention. I carefully drew a line between work and me. Yes, I screwed up the hero project of the year, but so what? I still deserve to live with dignity. I still can be happy. I should appreciate that the failure helped me win my life back.

Becoming a Giver

Before the trip to London, I was narrow-minded. If something went wrong, I tended to complain to others. When my colleagues and I got together, we were always gossiping—who got bullied, which executives said what, who got promoted, how bonuses were allocated, and so on.

After the trip, I changed. I realized that happiness is not about what you have but about what you give.

At work, in addition to my own duty, running a phone project, I joined the reorganization committee, to help redefine and document our process. While doing that, I gained more confidence because I saw my value at work and understood why I was suffering. I tried too hard to control everything, even in fields I'm not good at (like radio design details). When I was blamed for bad radio performance, I suffered and tried harder. I forgot I had a team with the best talents and, as a project manager, I should focus more on the whole picture and get the best resources to solve an issue.

This change in attitude spilled over to my family. My time with my family has increased. My parents are now old, and the news from the family is mostly sad as their health deteriorates. Dad's cancer has spread and he can't travel far these days, so I'm so grateful to have so many happy memories with my family during the 5 years from 2010 to 2014 while he was still healthy. Fortunately, I have the photos from those times to comfort me, and there have been many times when looking at them has cheered me up.

Besides work and family, I started to read all kinds of news, which has helped me gain a broader mind and a bigger vision. There are so many big issues in this world—hunger, refugees, wars, and more. Compared to those big things, my problems pale in comparison. During this time, I also discovered Kiva.org, a micro-lending platform, that makes me feel that I'm doing something meaningful with my money.

I've also noticed that there is no need to wait until there is money to help others. There are so many ways today to provide help and support to others. With a resource like Kiva, just $25 is enough to change the fate of a person or even a community.

Being a giver makes me feel good. As I began to look away from myself and see what I can do for others, my spirits improved, my life began to feel like it had a purpose. I no longer felt so needy.

I had always been a perfectionist. My familiarity with the process, mastery of the nature of things, the priority of the order, the clarity of the report—everything had to be perfect. But with this new view of life, I started to see that, for a lot of things, it didn't matter how well I did them but how I reacted to them.

I learned to cherish my life and be grateful, knowing that I have the ability to give. As a result, everything I do has value.

Loving Myself

So many years have passed, yet every time I think of 2007–2010, I still can't help crying. Not because the pain is still there; instead, these are grateful tears. I so appreciate what I've learned and received during my difficult days, especially one special friend. He was always there for me.

What did he do to help me through the lowest points of my life?

He is a wise man. I call him wise not because he gave me any specific piece of advice. Actually, we never discussed details of my failure at work. I call him wise because he did a far more important thing. He taught me to love myself.

He was simply by my side and kept saying, "Julia, you are great. Everything will be okay." We didn't talk much about what happened at my work, but he noticed that I was depressed and often used negative words to describe myself. Every time I criticized myself in front of him, he would repeat, "Julia, you are great."

In the beginning, when I heard him say, "Julia, you are great. Everything will be okay," I didn't think he meant it. I thought he just said that because he was my friend and he wanted to make me feel better.

Gradually, as he kept repeating, "Julia, you are great. Everything will be okay," I started to believe him, and my inner strength began to grow little by little. I changed the habit of blaming all the faults on myself. I paid attention to the facts instead.

When the whole world seems to be against you, it feels so d**n good when someone supports you unconditionally. Even now, every time I talk about him, I am still touched by the unconditional love he gave. It was so profound and beautiful! Thank you, W.

My Second Life

Since we were young, we have been taught to "pursue." Most people have never learned how to let go. However, if you keep holding on to the way things have been, nothing will change.

Look at the design of our hands. Only by releasing your hand are you able to accept anything. We must first let go before we take things. Sometimes, destiny is against us, things don't happen as we expect, and we can't control all the things that happen to us, no matter how hard we try. So, don't hold on too tight. Let go, and you will see opportunities are everywhere.

People tend to think that you have to succeed first, then consider giving back to others. However, according to the book *Give and Take*, the people we love most are givers. Most people think that "giving is to offer something to others," but often you will find that giving is to give back to yourself. For example, praise others, and you will get a smile back from others. Giving makes givers happy.

The Irish poet and playwright, Oscar Wilde, once said: "Loving yourself is the beginning of a lifelong relationship." Don't wait for others to fill up your cup, and don't just dedicate yourself fully to others' agendas. If you can fill up the cup in front of yourself and feel happy and satisfied, you will naturally be able to share the blessing of that full cup with others.

Let go, be a giver, and love yourself. These three things have formed the foundation of my life, they have turned my work into play, and they are the collateral beauty of my darkest days. How will you use them?

Julia (Hsingju) Tseng is a brave soul, loving traveling and expanding self's boundaries. With a background in physics and a Master's of Business Administration from the #1 university in Taiwan, National Taiwan University, Julia has rich experience in Engineering Project Management, Business Development, and Operation Management in the Smartphone and VR industries. After meeting Janet Bray Attwood and Chris Attwood, the founders of The Passion Test, Julia is also a Life Changer, impacting many people in Taiwan through conducting Passion Test Workshops and reading clubs. Julia's mission is to inspire and empower people to live in passion and happiness. In addition, Julia is an active volunteer for the Asian Classics Input Project, helping the preservation of ancient Asian wisdom. Contact Julia Tseng at jutseng@ gmail.com.

Chapter 9
THE ART OF MAKING WISE CHOICES

by Isa Zhang (China)

....

The American writer, Barbara De Angelis, once told a story in her book, *How Did I Get Here?*

A young man came to a small town and he felt thirsty. He saw a red, plump fruit in a convenience store and it looked delicious. He gave the owner money, and the owner gave him a large basket of fruit. He felt that he had made a great deal, so he sat on the side of the road and began to eat the fruit.

When he took the first bite of the fruit, he felt like he had a fire in his mouth, and it was so hot and sore that he almost died. However, he did not stop there.

When a passerby saw the young man suffering, he asked: "What are you doing?"

The young man answered: "This is the fruit I just bought. I thought they were delicious."

Passersby said: "These are red peppers. Eating too much will kill you."

The young man replied: "I will finish the last one because I am not eating chili, I'm eating my money."

While this story is funny and exaggerated, such examples are not uncommon in life. How many people, while complaining that their work is trivial and boring, are also reluctant to give up the income brought by their job, and stay at it, even when they don't enjoy it? How many mothers, while wanting the poetry of a beautiful future, can't get rid of their own psychological concept of being a model mother at the same time?

Making wise choices that bring you joy is the essence of what life is about. Yet most people have never learned how to do that. One who has impressed me deeply is my friend Miss Yu.

Miss Yu is an MD and discovered that she did not like being a doctor after working in a medical institution for two years. So, she left her prestigious position and opened a coffee shop. Now she owns two coffee shops. Because her coffee shop business is so successful, she is often invited to share her experience in business collaboration meetings. One of the most frequently asked questions she gets is: "Don't you feel it is a waste for an MD to go open a coffee shop?"

Miss Yu's reply? "If I start pursuing my favorite career now, I've only wasted the years I spent studying to become a doctor, but if I give up my favorite career and do something I don't like to do, then I've wasted my entire life."

Behind Miss Yu's answer is not only a reflection of wisdom but also a clear expression of her self-awareness. At the crossroads of life, making the right choice is not easy. Otherwise, there would be no such thing as confusion, indecision, and anxiety when I wonder whether I made a wrong decision. However, when you make the right choice, you feel a different energy.

How do you determine what is the right choice?

Have you ever experienced the feeling of being awakened by dreams in the morning? Perhaps it was a time you got a university admission notice. Perhaps it was a time when you changed your career track and were about to start a new life, or maybe it was a time when you loved your work so much that you stayed up the whole night.

The American basketball player, Kobe Bryant, told a story about waking at 4:00 in the morning that is a familiar to many of us:

A reporter asked Kobe: "What makes you so successful?"

Bryant answered: "Do you know what Los Angeles looks like at half-past four in the morning?"

The reporter shook his head.

Bryant said: "I know what Los Angeles looks like at half-past four every day."

Kobe Bryant loved his work so much that he rose before dawn to get an early start on every day.

This story is just like a phrase in the ancient Chinese poem, "Without the continuous bitter cold, there can be no fragrant plum blossoms." The bitter cold may not feel good in the moment, but the fruits it gives are sweet. As a result, even in the bitter cold, there is a gift. The motivation to act is driven by the love of what one is doing even when perseverance and difficult tasks are required. But how can you maintain such persistence when it may take several years for your actions to bear fruit?

In May 2014, I was in charge of a training program for my company. One day, at 4:00 in the morning, I was still in a taxi, between the printing factory and the training room, preparing the training materials to be used in a few hours. Recalling Kobe's story, I talked to myself silently: "I have seen this city at 4:00 in the morning." Despite the fact that I stayed up the whole night, suddenly I was invigorated, the tiredness was swept away. I believed that one day in the future, that picture would be frozen in my memory and I could cherish it as something precious, as I do now.

I remember that in the first year after graduation, I saw a particularly attractive work opportunity while I was presenting a proposal to a client. So, I began a series of consecutive overnight studies to create a PowerPoint describing how I was the perfect choice for this position and my plan for how to accomplish it. After three months, the proposal I submitted was accepted without modification.

During these months, at one time I had not been sleeping for 48 hours and then fell asleep in the taxi in the early morning. The taxi driver stopped at the entrance to the residential area where I lived for more than half an hour. He said he couldn't bear to wake me up because I was so tired. When I heard his words, tears streamed down my face. I was so touched by his thoughtfulness. These pictures are so clear in my mind, it seems that they just happened yesterday, but the happiness of tears with laughter was far greater than the memories of crying.

When I think of these things, my heart is full because no matter at which time, no matter what kind of things I face, humility and awe give me enthusiasm for life.

The lesson is that making the right choice comes from connecting deep inside yourself with that place where your tears of joy arise. The right choice, when faced with major life decisions, is the choice that touches your heart most deeply.

How do you make the right choice?

The Viva La Vida Club advocates the combination of knowledge, practice, and health as the core of life. Their view is that once we were immaculate. God then arranged a game for us, breaking the perfection into parts and implanting broken, incomplete beliefs, setting out different scenarios, problems, and difficulties so that we can indulge in this world of true and false, without a way back. Only when you open yourself to feel and experience life fully will you gradually become clear about your talents and passions and return to the present moment where you encounter your true self.

The *New York Times* bestselling authors, Janet and Chris Attwood, have created a tool called The Passion Test that has helped countless people figure out their top passions deep inside and expose the meaning of their life.

When you live in passion every day, what will you be like?

Last weekend, I met a girlfriend I hadn't seen in half a year. We had lunch and afternoon tea together. When we were about to say goodbye, she said to me: "From the moment I saw you, your eyes have the curve of the crescent moon, and the corners of your mouth have been raised up. Every time we meet, your passion infects me. We need to meet up more often."

On the same day, I met my English teacher, Amber, in the evening. When we chatted, she asked me: "How do you have passion for your work for years on end? You're still so happy, as if you will never get tired."

I said, "Because I love it. My work makes me happy." She still seems puzzled.

When Amber asked me that question, I didn't realize that the "passion" she talked about was actually a passion of mine. In the past, learning English was a kind of "stress" for me. I seemed to be relying on my willpower to force myself to "work hard on English." One day I suddenly realized that I have a picture of my passion inside: I'm talking to people in fluent English. Well, before this picture is fully realized, I must prepare my "props," i.e., fluent spoken English. After this awareness, the English class became fun and interesting for me as if it were magic. I'm waiting for the picture of my passion to appear in the near future, just like making tea at home waiting for a long-awaited friend, full of joy.

When you live in your passions every day, what would you be like?

You are peaceful.

You are joyful.

I always have the following sentence written in my notebook: "Life may have only one kind of success, that is, to spend your whole life in the way you like." Dreams coming true is what we all want. But how do you choose your own life, so that you have a calm and happy day every day?

As I think of this, I can't wait to share with you three techniques for making good choices:

1. Think positively and put in your cosmic order with the universe.
2. Break down your goals and formulate implementation strategies.

3. Pay attention to self-management and continuously optimize through regular evaluation.

Among these three techniques, the first one seems to be simple, but it is not easy to implement. Each of us can probably find many things that we don't want at any given time. For example: I don't want to be fat; I don't want to quarrel with my partner; I don't want to have a low income, but I don't want to work too hard every day either.

If you often have such thoughts, why not try to turn them around? The language may be like: I want to have a slim figure; I want to have a good relationship with my partner; I want to enjoy my work and be wealthy.

Writer Wallace Wattles wrote in his book *The Science of Getting Rich*: "You should have all the good things that life must give you: health, money, relationships, and life. To have a wealthy and abundant life is the birthright of everyone."

He advocates that "the things you want are originally yours, as long as the attraction is strong enough." The Law of Attraction has provided countless times of fulfillment for me. For example: Three years ago, I was still a rookie who was nervous every time I spoke on the stage. I met a teacher at work. My eyes widened at the sight of his lecture style. I felt for the first time that a person can shine with dazzling light on the stage, and I can feel the beauty of this radiance. At that time, I thought, how wonderful it will be if I can become someone like him. So, I took speaking courses, learning pronunciation and hosting skills. Now, I have given more than 200 speeches, and some were to thousands of people.

Two years ago, I started running. The process of running itself is boring. So, what I think about while I am running is that if I can run a marathon one day, what a bright life experience it will be. My mind is filled with countless scenes of running on the marathon track, and with countless pictures about how I am sharing my marathon experience with friends. Two years later, I completed two marathons, making those pictures real.

A half year ago, when I was on a business trip, I took a taxi to the airport. When I got out of the taxi, I left my mobile phone in the car. I contacted the taxi driver immediately when I found my phone was lost. When the driver got the call, he denied that he had my phone. I felt this was unbelievable, but at the same time, I thought he is a very young driver, and it's understandable if he has a moment of greed.

Nonetheless, my thoughts on the airplane were that my mobile phone was definitely forgotten in the taxi. The driver just doesn't want to return it to me for the time being, and he will return it to me eventually. I also imagined the scene, "After the mobile phone was found, I told people about this magical experience, how I lost and found my phone on the way to the airport." Then, a miracle happened. Just after the airplane landed, I received a text message from the taxi driver: "Your phone was found, give me the address and I will ship it back to you." So, after 72 hours of separation from the phone, the phone returned to me again.

With the goal created from mindful thinking, you can go to the second step and break down the implementation steps: Who is your hero—that person you admire? What qualities of him or her attract you? If your hero's status is 100, what score are you right now? What is the difference between you and him or her? How long do you need, and what do you need to do, in order to reach his or her status?

Here, your hero is our point of reference. We don't intend to copy another person's life. But when you have a clear goal, you not only act better but also, in the process of implementation, you will continue to surpass yourself based on the picture you have created in your mind.

The third technique is self-management. Just as no one will give you a written script of your whole life, you make your own life based on the choices you make and the actions you take every single day.

The first principle of self-management is never put off 'till tomorrow what you can do today. Just like "placing a cosmic order with the universe," you can create anything you want. The key point is, after you place a cosmic order with the universe, have you fulfilled your promise to pay the corresponding cost (including time and energy) to fulfill the order?

Each of us has only one life. In this life script, you are the protagonist. What kind of story do you want to tell?

Isa Zhang was born in August, 1984 in Shandong, China and currently lives in Beijing. Isa is a psychological counselor and a professional manager in consulting services. She is also a practitioner of Time Management and Lean Thinking, advocating high-efficiency and a multidimensional life. Isa has a long-term commitment to using entrepreneurship to explore the path of life and wealth freedom. She loves to read, write, and run marathons. Contact Isa Zhang at isazhang11@163.com or Wechat (ID: isa_cheung).

Chapter 10

4 STEPS TO FIND YOUR PATH TO HAPPY

By Julia Cain (USA)

....

Winter 1997 . . . Springfield, MA

Flee or die? Run away or kill myself?

I sat in the dark driveway, inside my parked car, listening to the sound of the angry rain violently pounding on my car, and considered the question.

Flee or die?

As I sank deeper and deeper into the debilitating pain of hopelessness and helplessness—my life feeling out of control—I couldn't think of any other way I could escape this anguish. Be dead or be gone felt like the only viable options.

Not knowing how much longer I could go on living in this pain, with no glimmer of hope in sight, I was sinking hard and fast into a dark and bottomless pit of despair.

With every ounce of my energy drained, my body slumped over with a deep sigh, as I dropped my forehead onto the steering wheel.

Would being dead offer me the escape I yearned for? Escape from the pain and desolation I had suffered for so long? Would running away offer the relief I so desperately craved?

With hope and happiness sucked out of my life, there was nothing good left. If this empty, frustrating, disappointing, and meaningless life really is all there is, I don't want it.

I knew I should get out of the car and go into the house. But why? I'd rather be dead than go in that house. I had been depressed and exhausted—physically, mentally, emotionally, and spiritually— for so long I had no memory of what "normal" felt like. "Normal" was no longer a dream to which I could aspire.

Through the car windshield, I could see lights shining cheerfully from the house windows—lights blurred from the tears flowing down my cheeks, blurred from the rain beating against the car windows.

I'm sure my husband and three young children were impatiently waiting for me to get home to make them dinner.

"God forbid my husband should get up off the couch and lift a finger around the house," I mumbled angrily to myself. He considered housework of any type beneath him. The house was always a mess and was falling apart due to lack of attention and maintenance.

I didn't have the energy to get out of the car and trudge into the house (a messy, falling-apart house I had grown to despise over the years), let alone find the energy to make dinner. I knew I wouldn't be able to start dinner until I cleaned up the sink full of dishes I was sure to find waiting to surprise me.

For the years I'd known him, my husband hadn't been successful keeping a full-time job, so it was my obligation to support the family. For the most part, he stayed home with the kids most of the day—killing time playing video games.

And here I am, just getting home after a demanding 12-hour workday at the restaurant and—because of the crappy weather—battled traffic for another 45 minutes, and I knew my husband's expectation would be for me make dinner and then bathe the kids and put them to bed.

"What is wrong with me? Why am I putting up with this?" I exclaimed crossly to myself as tears continued to stream down my cheeks.

Seven years into a disappointing marriage, I kept asking myself "Why does it have to be this way?"

The more I thought about it, the angrier and more irritated I got. The tears were no longer tears of anguish and despair. These were tears of frustration and anger.

My life sucked, and I loathed it. I wanted out and I didn't care how.

What if I did run away from home? Disappear into the night? Maybe I could just keep driving until I got to the other side of the country.

That night, so close to the edge of leaving it all behind, the only thing that held me back was the thought of my three beautiful, magical children. I was so in love with them. They were the only real spot of sparkling joy in my ugly, cheerless, and unhappy life.

Thoughts of my children protected the only piece of happiness that hadn't been sucked away by the evil and foul dementors that seemed to surround me.

Suddenly a thought occurred to me; I sat up straight, the steady stream of tears shutting off abruptly, like a water faucet being turned off.

"Am I feeling sorry for myself?" I questioned. This was like a slap in the face! My dad taught me better than that. He always said, "You gotta carry your own weight in this life Jules. Nobody is going to do it for you. Take control of your own life. When you give over control to anyone else for any reason, you become powerless. Carry your own weight."

Did I give away my control, my power? Is that why I feel helpless and frustrated? Did I allow this situation to happen? Did I create this circumstance that seemed to hem me in on all sides?

I was the one who said yes when my future husband asked me to marry him. I was pregnant, and even though I knew at some deep level marrying him was wrong, I did it anyway.

I was the one who chose to stay in a job I hated. It felt like I was trapped since I was the one supporting the family financially. Why was I pretending I had no choice?

I had allowed my husband and others to dictate who I should be, what I should do, and how I should behave. Sitting there in the car, I knew that I was completely responsible for my current life and circumstances.

If I was responsible and I had created, promoted, or allowed the things that had created my current situation and circumstances, couldn't I un-create it by making different decisions, different choices? I knew I had the power to make different decisions, but did I have the courage?

If it was true that I had the power and courage, then fleeing into the night or wishing myself dead was probably not the best decision for me to make.

When I was growing up, my father was in the US Air Force (20+ years), so our family spent a lot of time living in countries outside of the U.S. When my dad retired and the family settled in Lucas Valley, California (a small neighborhood in Marin County, just north of San Francisco), I had a very difficult time adjusting to my new peers who had grown up and gone to school together. It never quite felt like I belonged there during those school years. In the middle of this awkward adjustment, my parents decided to divorce. This was a devastatingly painful time for me, and I ended up turning to drugs and other ways to numb the pain.

Over the intervening years, I experienced a long period of heroin addiction, several periods of homelessness, and more visits to jails, prisons, and rehab centers than I can count.

So, if I had successfully conquered years of heroin addiction, survived several years in prison and homelessness, shouldn't I be able to survive ending an unhappy marriage and quitting a soul-crushing job—both of which were sucking the life out of me?

By this time, I was married, enjoying a somewhat successful corporate career, had a house (with a mortgage), 3 children, took vacations, and had a little money in savings. By definition, I had achieved the American dream. Right?

So why did I feel so empty, so hopeless, so helpless, so lost?

Sitting in that parked car, in the dark, rainy driveway I considered this new "prison" I had created for myself: stuck in an unhappy marriage, living in a house I didn't like, barely tolerating the unpleasant weather, spending most of my waking hours working at a soul-crushing job, and too exhausted at the end of the day to enjoy time with my children.

Is this who I want to be for the rest of my life?

It was in that moment I knew I was being treated exactly as I had expected to be treated. In that moment, my evolution began. I knew for sure what I *didn't* want! I was committed to change my circumstances and my life, but before I could *do* anything, I needed to decide what I *did* want.

I wanted to:

- live somewhere the weather was pleasant year-round;
- do meaningful and fulfilling work that could support us financially;
- spend more time with my children;
- end the unhappy and unfulfilling marriage with my husband;
- finish the bachelor's degree I had been working toward for so many years.

Knowing the path ahead was not going to be an easy one, I still had a burning desire to create the new life I wanted.

Feeling anxious and afraid, acknowledging the risk and the potential for failure, I was committed to changing my life. Even the possibility of failure was better than staying stuck where I was. Anything was better than what I was leaving behind.

I left Massachusetts in May of 1998 and have never looked back.

During my personal evolution on this journey, I have experienced feelings of joy and happiness that were unimaginable for me during that dark time in 1997. I have also experienced times of sadness, frustration, and struggle. I've veered off track more than once, but, because I knew exactly what I wanted, it was easier to get back on track.

My life is not perfect. I still occasionally struggle with fear, depression, and disillusionment, but in the years since I left Massachusetts, my story continues to evolve.

I continue to take full responsibility for everything in my life. No more blaming. No more complaining. Well . . . most of the time, and now I am more aware when I am blaming and complaining and feeling triggered by someone or something. When I am aware that I am giving my power to someone or something outside of me, it gives me the ability to make different decisions. Awareness gives me choices.

As I continue on this path of growth and change, my passions and career choices continue to evolve with me. Between 2006 and 2018, I was doing work that I loved, with a company I loved, and surrounded by a brilliant team I loved. Together we designed and built creative custom software solutions that efficiently and effectively solved HR and business problems. I loved this work! I loved it . . . until I didn't love it anymore.

The money was great; the team was great; I was successful professionally and financially. It would have been easy and comfortable to stay. But I wasn't happy anymore. I was no longer fulfilled, no longer satisfied. It was time for me to do something scary again. I had to leave.

I would have been living a lie if I had stayed just because it was safe, secure, easy, and comfortable. So, I left in January of 2019 and started my own business. And now every day is a new adventure, a new puzzle to solve! I am alive again!

I did have to find the courage to change my path without fully knowing where it was going or what I was doing. When I realized that I didn't need to know the whole path before I could take a step, I took the step. Then the next step showed up, so I took it. Then the next one. Then the next.

Today I still start right where I am, and I take the next step that shows up. Even if I'm not sure what the step after that one might be, I take the next step. The uncertainty of where I'm going is scary at times, and I'm doing it anyway. Every day I wake up excited to see what gifts the day will bring!

The secret of success

"A wise man said the secret of success comes in three parts.

"First, decide what you want to do. Most people have no idea.

"Second, decide what you are prepared to give up to do it. Most people aren't willing to make real sacrifices.

"And the third part? Do it. Most people just talk about doing something—and that's as far as it gets."

Drayton Bird

Carry My Own Weight

"In the long run, we shape our lives, and we shape ourselves. The process never ends until we die. And the choices we make are ultimately our own responsibility."

Eleanor Roosevelt

In order to believe that your life can be different, you must first believe that you are responsible for where you are in your life. That *you* have created, promoted, or allowed the life you currently have. When you fully own responsibility for where you are, that awareness creates a realization that you also have the power to change it. You can create a different life.

It seems like the world is teaching us that when something is not right in our life, we need to quickly blame someone or something outside of ourselves. That person or that thing needs to change in order for us to be happy.

Are we being conditioned to believe that we have no control and power over our own circumstances?

We need only to listen to the news for a few minutes to know that everything wrong in our lives is because of:

President Trump
The Pope
Republicans
Democrats
Foreign Policy
Economy

Boss

Coworkers

Parents

Spouse

Millennials

Old people

Men

Women

Who do you blame?

When you are triggered, then fall into the trap of "blaming and complaining," you continue to allow external forces to have power and control over your life and how you feel. You have given up your power. I challenge you to take your power back! Consciously create the life you desire. Step away from blaming and complaining and take responsibility for your current life results.

If you aren't happy, change your response to the situation or event. Do something different. Take action to change the situation. Don't just complain about it; take action. While you can't change external events, you can change how you respond to those events, and, in your response, you can change your outcomes.

> *"Everything can be taken from a man but one thing: the last of the human freedoms—to choose one's attitude in any given set of circumstances, to choose one's own way."*
>
> *Viktor E. Frankl,* Man's Search for Meaning

I Know What I Don't Want . . . What the Heck Do I Want?

"I had to decide what I was going to do, and what I was going to be. I was standing there, waiting for someone to do something, till I realized the person I was waiting for was myself."
Markus Zusak

It's pretty easy to know what you don't want because the thing you don't want is probably causing you some pain in your life. It could be a job, a relationship, financial worries, lack of direction in life, or knowing something is missing but not sure what it is.

Coaching clients I've worked with over the years seem to share a similar theme: their career/job chose them; they didn't make a thoughtful choice. Then they stayed in that career/job because it was easy, comfortable, and paid the bills. At some point, they realized one day, that while they were "successful" in the traditional sense, they felt unfulfilled, like something was missing in their lives, but they weren't sure what it was or how to find it.

One of the top reasons most people don't get what they want is because they haven't really identified what they do want. They let life or someone else decide for them, all the while continuing to complain about what they currently have.

Take the next step:

- Decide what you want. Write it down.
- Make a plan (set goals). Figure out what you need to do to get there. (I wanted a degree. I had to register for the classes I

needed to complete the degree. Then I determined how long it would take so I could have a realistic expectation.)

- Then take action. Do something every day that will bring you closer to what you want.

You will never leave where you are until you decide where you would rather be.

> *"You have brains in your head. You have feet in your shoes. You can steer yourself in any direction you choose. You're on your own, and you know what you know. And you are the one who'll decide where to go."*
>
> **Dr. Seuss**

How on Earth Do I Get There from Here?

> *"The trouble with not having a goal is that you can spend your life running up and down the field and never score."*
>
> **Bill Copeland**

Once you have a clear picture in your mind of what you want, you can use goal setting to move your vision into reality. Converting your vision into goals will keep you focused on the action steps that will move you closer to the life you want to create.

Many people have never set goals for a number of reasons, some of which are noted below:

Don't know how, never taught

Discouraged or laughed at by others when they set goals

Fear of being rejected
Fear of failing

To make a goal a reality, the goal should:

- be specific and measurable
- be believable to you
- be communicated to others
- have a time limit
- have internal and external roadblocks accepted as a natural part of the journey

Setting goals activates both the conscious and the subconscious mind to figure out what needs to happen to make that goal a reality. When you put a time limit, it makes it even more powerful.

"I wrote it down, put a date on it, listed the obstacles I had to overcome, identified the people, the groups, the organizations I needed to work with, spelled out a plan of action, set that time limit in there, and identified all the benefits to me. It was only when I did that, that the goal became a reality."
Zig Ziglar

Find the Courage and Do It!

"Start where you are. Use what you have. Do what you can."
Arthur Ashe

Starting can be the hardest part. So many people know what they want but never take the next step toward their desire. Or stop when it gets too hard or uncomfortable.

The world doesn't pay you for what you know; it pays you for what you do. So many of us get bogged down in analyzing, planning, and organizing, or thinking we need something more before we get started. We need to be perfect before we can start. In truth, all we need to do is take action. Start where you are and take action.

When you take action, you trigger all kinds of things that will inevitably carry you to success. You are communicating your goals to people around you, and your action lets them know you are serious in your intention to achieve this goal. You will likely find that people with similar intentions or goals become aligned with you.

By taking action, you will begin to learn things from your experience that can't be learned by taking another class or seminar, reading another book, or watching other people take action. In taking action, you will begin to get feedback about what works and what doesn't, how to do it better, how to do it quicker. Without taking action, you will remain stuck right where you are.

One secret to getting started is to break your complex and overwhelming goals or tasks into smaller and more manageable tasks, then start the first one.

Without movement, nothing happens. You become stagnant, stuck in the same place. One small step, one small shift in your perspective can move you forward in amazing ways. You don't need to see the whole path before you start. Take the step.

It might be scary. Do it anyway.

"The secret to starting is to . . . just start. The path to success is a series of small achievable actions and tasks."
Julia Cain

4 Steps You Can Take to Find Your Path to Happy

"The only way to do great work is to love what you do. If you haven't found it yet, keep looking. Don't settle. As with all matters of the heart, you'll know it when you find it."
Steve Jobs

1. Carry your own weight.
2. Get clear on what you want.
3. Action Plan: Create goals that get you from here to there.
4. Start where you are and take action.

If you would like an opportunity for a 30-minute free consultation to walk through these steps and how to apply them to your personal situation, you may schedule time with me at the following link: https://calendly.com/cainconsulting/findyourhappy

I would also love to share my next 10-Day Happiness Challenge with you. Happiness seems so simple, yet it evades so many of us. From being stopped by fear and negative thoughts to expecting happiness from external rewards, we're all guilty of forgetting how to tap into happiness.

If you would like to sign up for my next 10-Day Happiness Challenge, please email me at julia@cainconsultingservices.com and I will alert you a couple of days before the next challenge starts. When the challenge starts, you will get one daily email from me during those 10 days. You will also have the opportunity to participate in a private forum with other participants during the challenge.

The financial cost to you: zero. The benefit of being able to access happiness on demand: priceless.

> *"When I was 5 years old, my mother always told me that happiness was the key to life. When I went to school, they asked me what I wanted to be when I grew up. I wrote down 'happy.' They told me I didn't understand the assignment, and I told them they didn't understand life."*
>
> **John Lennon**

Julia Cain works with people who want to improve their quality of life in the areas of career/job, relationships, and finances. With more than 25 years of experience guiding people from every occupation, Julia instructs people on simple, yet powerful, systems for personal and professional transformation that are innovative, practical, easy to use, and can create meaningful and positive changes in their lives. By using proven techniques and using examples of her own highly successful experiences, Julia will show you how to live the life you dream of. She teaches practical steps and strategies for improving quality of life in areas such as: how to set meaningful goals and achieve them, turn obstacles into opportunities, rid yourself of guild and inner turmoil, develop unshakable confidence, dramatically improve relationships, and spend your days doing things you love.

Chapter 11

FINDING HARMONY . . .
IN WORK AND LIFE

By Kyoko Kazemichi (Japan)

....

"Okay Shylock, I will allow you to cut off one pound of meat from Antonio's chest."

As Shylock grabbed Antonio's chest and pressed his knife against it, Portia said: "Now wait. This bond permits you to cut off one pound of meat. Exactly one pound. Not any more or less. And you cannot let blood spill—not even one drop. It doesn't say anywhere in here that you are allowed to spill blood."

The audience took a breath of relief as they watched this intense scene play out on stage.

"Great, that's great everybody. You are all great actors!" I told them.

127

This was my class of 12 grade-five students, and I was very proud of them. They had come to me three years after the devastating 2011 earthquake in East Japan that destroyed a nuclear power plant. Fearful of the effects of radiation on their children, many parents transferred their kids to out-of-town schools like mine, far away from the catastrophe.

Probably like yours, my life has been a struggle at times to find a balance between work and the rest of my life. In this chapter, let me use the experience with my students to share an insight with you that can help you resolve the apparent conflict between work and life so you can move easily in the flow of your life.

I love teaching and, with such a small class, I was able to bring out each student's uniqueness and the teaching was very fulfilling for me.

Drama allows a teacher to help students improve their language skills, both their expression and their comprehension. It requires that students understand the thinking process of each character and step into their emotions. Then they have to figure out how to express that.

I gave the class several suggestions for the play they'd perform, and, from these, they chose Shakespeare's *The Merchant of Venice*. The play was re-written to make it easier for these Japanese students to understand.

Shylock, the leading role in this play, was a Jewish loan shark, and it was the perfect role for one of my students. But this student was bigger than the other children and had challenges accepting himself.

Earlier, he and I had a chance to work together in a way that helped build his self-esteem. Three months after I became the teacher for these 12 children, there was a district carnival that gathered all the primary schools in the district.

Most schools chose their very fastest runners to compete in the relay race. But the relay required four runners and that's all we had. One of those runners was this big boy who was not the fastest runner by a long shot.

For quite some time I thought about how to organize this small team of runners so they could perform at their best. How could we smash through our disadvantaged circumstances when other schools had many runners to choose from?

"Not enough students to make a selection. Students that cannot run very well. What was the best time of the fastest runner on a 100-meter track? Who has the longest strides?" These were the thoughts running through my head. On and on it went, while I was cooking dinner . . . while having a bath . . . at school . . . at home.

The job of a teacher isn't something that you can just shut off when you finish your workday. "Working hours" is just a concept.

So, I thought everything through; I had repeated discussions with my colleagues who know athletics well, and I ran out to the schoolyard as soon as my last class ended to test out my theories and then took that into our practice.

Usually, in a relay race, the next runner starts running in the relay zone as the current runner runs up to pass the baton. However, knowing that our student with the bigger body was not a strong long-distance runner, we arranged for his next runner to wait at the line instead of taking the head start.

We placed a tall boy who had the longest legs and the fastest speed to take over as the next runner for this big guy. Since he couldn't get a running start, we guided him to use his wide steps and strong legs to push himself forward as quickly as possible.

We showed these students how to use their minds to help them run as fast as possible and, in the end, they beat out many other schools to nab third place. They got a bronze medal and they were so thrilled!

The team never excluded the big boy with the least running abilities, but instead, they said, "It was because of him that we could participate in the relay." As a result, he felt part of the victory and valued as part of his team.

All the while, I was thinking of a way to bring this boy's true power to the forefront and decided to do this at the student drama showcase.

So, I cast this boy as the lead character, Shylock. From his external appearance to his ability to express, this was the ideal role for this boy to excel.

In preparation for the drama showcase, I transformed myself into a stage director, to learn how best to bring out this boy's talents. I was able to attend the *Merchant of Venice* adapted to and performed by one of the best Kabuki theatres.

If I'm going to do something, I take a thorough approach. So, on Sunday, my day off, I jumped onto a bullet train to Tokyo. As I watched the play, I analyzed the performance: Right, it works to direct this scene like this. What sound effects are used? What is the set design like? How is Shylock portrayed? How are Portia's lines delivered in the court scene?

I went to see the play as a part of my duty as a school teacher, pushing aside my planned housework for that day, but I have been a fan of theatre and I was able to not only see it from a professional standpoint, but I was also able to enjoy the actor's talents and stagecraft. By bringing work with my own interests together, I was able to create the result I shared with you in the beginning.

Now I invite you to consider how these two examples illustrate the following principles and how you can apply them to your own life.

Work-Life Balance

I'm sure you have heard these words. In Japanese, it is translated as the harmony between work and life and it's getting a lot of attention as the way of being in this modern world.

Valuing the many faces we have

This can be said to be the secret to a happy life.

- Your "mom face" from your child's point of view
- Your "working face"
- Your "wife face" in your husband's eyes
- Your "daughter face" when around your parents
- The "daughter-in-law face" around your husband's family

And one more thing we must not forget

- Your face as a human being, as a woman—your "true face."

Many working women, especially mothers, have many faces, but no matter what face you are wearing, it is a very valuable thing in your life. If the balance of each face is well kept, your heart can remain stable as well.

The more you get to wear your own face, the more you will find you are able to hold more space in your heart and be able to treat your family and the people around you with kindness.

However . . .

When you are bringing up children who are toddlers and up to primary to junior high-school-age children, you'll often be wearing your "mom face." In the worst case, this may be the only face you wear in your everyday life. When you add work to that, it can get harder to hold space in your heart for yourself.

Now I invite you to grab a pen and paper.

Think about the last week. How often do you use each face in a day? What is the average?

What if you discover . . . my true face doesn't show up that much . . .

As I told you in the first half of this story, in my own experience as a teacher, I spent a lot of time wearing my "work face" while trying to help raise the academic abilities of my students and help them use their personal power.

If I look at it from a time management point of view, I am certainly off balance. But what if we see things from the perspective of stress management?

If you are not finding it stressful to integrate the time spent on both work and life, then I believe this can be a healthy way of living. This is thinking of "work as life."

No matter how much you adore and love your child, constantly wearing your "mom face" can lead to a build-up of stress, too. If the dad can then take over for a while so the mom can return to her "true face" to go shopping or to see her friends and experience excitement, that's one way to have a happy balance in life.

Seeing a play that is in both your professional and personal interest and filling up on excitement and tackling the household chores in one go later on in the day, that's another way to have a happy balance in life.

It may only be one example; however, even when I am trying to push my student's potential and as a result end up being my "work self" more than usual, if I can look for a way to make my work exciting and satisfying for myself, I'm able to find a way to bring back my work-life balance.

When I look at this from a higher perspective, over a longer period of time, I was able to see beyond my career as a teacher and what the next thing could be. This meant that I was able to see that even if my work and life became off balance momentarily, I am able to re-calibrate through looking at it from a stress management perspective.

This helped me realize that the key is not "balance," but harmony. When there is a harmonious relationship between your work and the rest of your life, then life flows easily.

So, I invite you to reflect on your life once again. You can have that happy harmony in your life, too.

Kyoko Kazemichi *was born in Tokyo and now lives in Fukushima Prefecture. For 38 years she's been an elementary school teacher, counseling and teaching more than 10,000 students and parents. After retiring as a school teacher, she founded the Kazemichi Institute for Education, continuing to serve as a counselor and educational advisor to parents and children. She is the author of* The Book That Saves My Child From Worrying About Friends *and a Passion Test Facilitator. After the Great East Japan Earthquake in 2011, Kyoko helped relieve the hearts of children who were psychologically damaged by the earthquake and nuclear power accident.*

Chapter 12

RISING FROM THE ASHES

By Brigida Lanzani (Argentina)

· ·

"At this very moment there are 1,500 souls sitting in this hall," said the presenter when he brought me up to the stage, and my heart skipped a beat. I saw that people were giving me a standing ovation and I couldn't believe it. Finally, I did it! I was living my passion. But let me go a couple of years back, to the moment when my life changed forever.

I was attending a seminar about meditation when the organizer said: "The speaker's flight will be two hours late due to the ashes . . . so, in the meantime, we will show you a motivational movie."

The ashes from a volcano located 1,800 km away covered the sky of Buenos Aires, and all flights had been cancelled. When I heard the announcement, I thought, "This day can't get worse." During the whole year, I had compulsively and desperately attended each and every course available and had seen each and every specialist I stumbled on, trying to find the way to make a change in my life. And now I had to wait two more hours?

That was a clear sign that I had to get up and leave. I grabbed my purse, stood up, and asked for permission to get out, when a phrase in the background got my attention: "What would you do today if you knew you couldn't fail?" I let myself fall on my chair. The question went through me like an icy sword that shook my soul. The next two hours would change my life forever.

For a moment, my mind went back through the moments of my life and stopped in those moments when I thought I could do anything. My memories took me to Formosa, a little lost town in the north of Argentina, where I grew up. Yuck! It had been a long time since I'd thought of my childhood. For a few moments, that felt like hours, my body sat still in the present; I could hear the movie in the background, but my thoughts went back to my childhood, when playing on the sidewalk and riding my bike were the things I loved the most. The days when I was a little girl passed by with the warmth of the tropical sun and the unconditional love of my parents. I was happy. At that time, I felt complete, and I felt able to win any battle. Failing wasn't an option; I was born to win. Innocence saved me from any bad thoughts. I was free.

When I was a teen, my family and I had to go back to live in Buenos Aires, and that was a turning point in my life, a watershed. My parents stopped getting along, and my mom stayed inside her bedroom for days. Dad traveled a lot, and daily life started to get complicated. Sometimes we can't remember the exact moment when we stop believing in ourselves, but I'm sure that for me it was during that time. The sad feelings behind those memories brought me back to the present.

Little by little I was coming back to the place where I was sitting. "When was the last time I believed in myself?" I thought, unable to find the answer.

A phrase I had once read crossed my mind: "We don't choose the circumstances; we choose our answer to the circumstances." And there I was, frozen in my chair in that hall full of strangers, waiting, without realizing that the very same volcano ashes covering the sky of Buenos Aires had caught me long ago. For the very first time, I started to see clearly. Glued to my chair, I wrote everything I would do if I knew I wouldn't fail on a piece of paper that I found inside my purse. The list looked never-ending. I would have a happy family, a marriage full of light, I would make decisions I had been procrastinating on, I would travel, and would have work I really love. As I wrote, time flowed by, and I felt one with the universe.

That day a new stage in my life started, when tired and defeated, almost to my 40s, I decided to assist with the meditation course my friend had told me about.

Up until then, a feeling of chronic anxiety inside my chest had been choking me. My marriage was in crisis. After fifteen years, constant fighting had eaten away at our relationship. The little energy left in me was being drained slowly away after each discussion. We were consuming each other in this battle of egos. Our few moments of peace were not enough. Despite my husband's loving and admiring eyes, always looking at me with care, their comfort was not enough, and the memories of our bitter moments were stronger. What united us as a couple was not as strong as the wounds we were causing each other. I needed to be alone, to fly away.

It was July, right in the middle of the school year in Argentina. Along with everything else I was going through, we had been summoned to school three times for our dear, eight-year-old son. The last thing we had heard from the school was: "Your son has traits of autism." He wasn't fitting in to the standards of a "regular" kid his age, according to the male chauvinist culture that surrounded us.

He hated football and loved science and the theatre. While his friends played soccer and wanted their favorite soccer team t-shirt, my son preferred a microscope or hunting ants in the garden. He couldn't tolerate studying and had adopted many different mechanisms to avoid doing his homework. His self-esteem was crumbling and there was only one option left for us: going against family tradition and moving him to another school. He needed a new environment that could value the wonderful person he was. "You are about to make the worst mistake of your lives!" my brother-in-law, a former student from this same school, told us. "All our sons have always attended this school and they always will; it is tradition."

"He is not able to keep up with the rest of the students; he is the last student to finish activities in class," his teacher used to tell us. The principal told us: "We will keep on trying for one more year and see if he can come up to the level of his classmates." Every parent conference made me question myself as a mother, and the family I had always dreamt of was falling to pieces. What was going on with my dream life that it was crashing down? Yet, I felt so numb that I had no reaction whatsoever. What was wrong with me?

"Have you ever tried meditating?" a friend asked me. At that moment, I was ready to try anything. I wanted to discover what it meant to heal oneself through introspection. The funniest thing about this is that it was not the course that changed my life, but something that happened during the waiting time before the course.

The room was full of people. A woman next to me was playing impatiently with the rings on her left hand, while a man with an empty look in a dark suit was checking his phone again and again. Diego, my husband, was sitting next to me; we had gone together but were not on good terms. At this point in our relationship, we were fighting about everything. We hadn't talked to each other since we had arrived at the place where the course would be held. The emptiness I felt inside was incomprehensible.

At that instant, my phone beeped. It was a text message from him, saying: "I prefer to maintain our relationship than be right." I stared directly into his eyes and we were suspended in time. It was a deep, profound moment that may have only lasted seconds, but it felt like hours. Neither of us had ever experienced such a thing before. We were standing here together. not because of chance, but because we wanted to be there with each other. That day, lost in his gaze, I was reborn from the ashes.

The sweetness in his eyes transported me through time, to the day I first met him. He always had faith in me, even when I did not. At that time, nothing felt easy for me; the melancholy and feeling of emptiness inside prevented me from spreading my wings. But by his side, I had always felt powerful.

What had happened to me? Deep inside I knew that I was destined for something great, but I couldn't find what it was. He had appeared in my life to make me believe that everything was possible, like the time when I lived in Formosa. Noble-hearted and self-assured, he dazzled me, taking my fears away and helping me stand strong. And there he was, sitting down next to me in that room, expecting to find a solution for our problems in this course.

Why was I living a life I did not want? What did I have to change? My energy had abandoned me long ago, and I was being a witness to the ending of everything I cared about. Depression had always haunted me like a shadow. My mother, my grandparents, and almost all my ancestors had suffered from it, but ever since I was young, I had decided I was not going to be another of its victims. I had always fought against falling into its claws, though many times I was close to succumbing to it.

My mother didn't share my fate; her depression became cancer and she passed away some years later. Adding to the pain of her loss, I had to suffer from a failing marriage and a son who could not fit in to the regular standards of society. My son's impending change of schools, the struggle against family tradition, and a relationship full of passion and hatred were slowly eating away at my lust for life. I was reluctant to end up like my mother and I constantly struggled with my inner storms. Was I going to fail in my marriage like my parents did in theirs? Was I going to force my son to adapt to the regular standards of society and family? Or was I going to accept reality and create a better response?

All these experiences had driven me to being in that room listening to those words, "What would you do today if you knew you couldn't fail?" One simple question that would change my entire life and perhaps can change yours as well.

As the motivational film came to an end, that exchange between my husband and me when we looked deeply into each other's eyes was imprinted deep in my heart. I was the protagonist in my own story, and that was what helped me out of my resignation.

From that moment on, I made motivation and coaching my lifestyle. I investigated it and studied. Nothing was ever the same after that grey Saturday covered in ashes. The idea of having been almost stopped by the fear of failing was a breaking point in my life. I moved my son to a new school, where he was valued for who he was and acknowledged for his inner light. He became admired by his classmates and a person everybody wanted to have around. A year later, at only nine-years-old, he told me: "Mum, now I am happy."

In addition, I had learned to have the necessary conversations with my husband and to return that loving gaze that had always been there. Together we managed to put our relationship before our egos. My husband and I became inseparable.

One change followed another one and the first results were noticeable, but still I needed to find my true passion.

I clearly remember when a book called *The Passion Test*, by Chris and Janet Attwood, came to me. In the middle of that spiritual search I had begun, coincidence now had a place. It was one holiday afternoon on the farm, bored with just resting and driven by that particular energy I had gained since that day when I'd heard that question that had never left me. I decided to start reading this book which I had postponed for too long.

"Passion is a very personal experience. When you start doing what you love, what you are really passionate about, your life will move irresistibly in directions that you cannot even begin to imagine," the authors said at the beginning of the second chapter. After two days of reading, I realized I wanted to complete the certification to become a facilitator of this Passion Test, the first facilitator in my country, and one of the few in South America. Being the best motivational speaker of my country, travelling around the world and being treated as a queen, writing a book of great international impact, cultivating my body and spirit, and renewing a good relationship were my main passions, and I had discovered them thanks to this simple test.

What is passion? That fire that always pulls you forward. My passions made me travel all over the world, getting to know top-level transformational speakers and learn from them. We must always have big dreams, because big dreams cause you to be surrounded by great people, and I can testify to that.

I traveled to places I never imagined I would ever visit. I walked on burning embers with Tony Robbins to prove to myself that I could go beyond my limiting beliefs. I came to know and learn from people like Jack Canfield and Janet Bray Attwood. As a facilitator, I delivered the Passion Test to more than 500 people in 1 year across my country and did almost 300 individual sessions that changed many lives. Sometimes we spend years looking for opportunities without realizing that life itself is an opportunity.

Which were the lessons that produced those changes in my life?

Overall, the most important thing is to listen to your heart. Sometimes it's hard to hear its whisper over our inner chatter, but it is your only inner source of wisdom. Courage is needed to follow your own path, realizing that you are responsible for what happens to you. Life is full of moments that can make the difference, but the person you can become in the process is more important than what you achieve.

We all have our dark side, corners inside that make us feel ashamed, frightened, and uncomfortable. We can't ignore them, but we can face them and learn from them.

The emotional connections lift us up and help us grow. Look for the good, interesting, and impressive in every person you relate to, so you will appreciate and understand them more. Success doesn't come from fighting against the obstacles and challenges but thanks to them.

My first passion, to be the best motivational speaker I am capable of, moved me to do things I didn't think I would be able to do before. I chose a goal so crazy it was like a dream: to host a conference and speak in front of 1,500 people. I knew that the day I succeeded I would feel I was living a passionate life. And it was like that. I registered myself as a speaker in the first Coaching and Neuroscience congress organized in my country and I was selected. There was no fear to fail inside me anymore.

"At this very moment there are 1,500 souls sitting in this hall," said the presenter when he brought me up to the stage. The rest is history. For the first time, I understood that when you align with your passions, your soul and your destiny align too, and this is the key to happiness.

Brigida Lanzani is a life coach and Passion Test facilitator. Her #1 passion is helping women to discover their best version of themselves. For this reason, she has studied with transformational leaders such as Janet and Chris Attwood, Jack Canfield, Patty Aubrey, and Tony Robbins. Brigida has been working with women for the last 10 years to help them unleash their potential and love their perfect imperfections through one-on-one coaching, weekend workshops, and trainings all over Argentina. She will soon publish her first book called: Perfectly Imperfect: Seven Steps to Stop Seeking Love, Approval and Appreciation from Others. *Brigida can be reached through Instagram at brigidalanzani.*

Chapter 13
RECOVERING FROM DISASTER

By Tomomi Tsukiyama (Japan)

The sound of feet walking over the gravel on the road to the shrine echoes, as my family walks in silence. Once through the Torii gate of the shrine, something in the air changes and the body tenses up. Yet, you also feel a certain sense of comfort, like you are being held by something.

On a hot summer's day, 13 years ago, we set off to climb Mount Miwa in Nara Prefecture with the very last of our hope. The mountain was just behind the approaching path of the Oomiwa Shrine. My father had failed in business and had a debt of more than 80 million yen (~$750,000), and we had just a month left until we were to lose everything, including our home and his job.

That terrible experience proved to be the doorway to discovering the amazing and wonderful life I now live. In this chapter, I hope to show you how your worst adversities can turn into your greatest blessings when you stay open.

Mount Miwa is said to be a manifestation of God's body, and Oomiwa Shrine that worships this mountain is said to be Japan's most ancient shrine. We had a curious connection to this shrine, and for eight years, my father and I visited the shrine as if we were led there by something. Whenever we would visit this shrine, somehow, we were given a helping hand from somewhere.

For my younger brother, this was the very first time he visited the Oomiwa Shrine. We had done everything we could possibly think of, so all we could do now was to pray. We decided to let the powers that be lead us. I was prepared to accept anything and everything, but somehow a part of me also believed in miracles: "I'm certain we'll be okay!"

A week later, a man visited my father's company. "When my father had just 6 months left to live from lung cancer," he said, "you were our guarantor and as a result, we got to keep our company from going bankrupt. A decade has passed since, and the business is going very well. Is there anything that I can do for you? I would like to repay the favor."

We just needed a place to live, so we bowed our heads as low as we could and asked him to buy our house. He accepted our request with just one word and bought our 60-million-yen home and land. He allowed us to pay rent and continue to live in our home.

The miracles did not stop there.

Even though we still owed millions to his company, the CEO of one of my father's clients offered to support us by doing business with my brother's new business. My brother had decided to start a new business in construction to support our family.

Although we had to sell the land that my grandparents left us, we got to keep our home. And even after that, people kept bringing business to my brother, all saying how much my father had helped them. My brother worked hard to gain trust from having less than nothing. And in just 5 years, we were able to buy back our home. His business is still going well.

With this, our family was united back together.

I had intended to help my brother with his business. However, he said, "You found something you want to do, I want you to make that your work." And from that year on, I began working as a spiritual counselor.

Growing up, I felt a sense of sadness as I was always in the care of my grandparents because both my parents were working. At age 11, my mother couldn't even recognize me as her daughter because of her mental illness. As a result, I was torn away from her. I experienced deep loneliness and shock. It took more than 20 years for me to heal.

My mother's condition sparked my initial interest in psychology. When she was taken away from me, I stuck my head in books about psychology, hoping to heal her illness, so I could see her smile again. People around us said that she would never get better, but I had faith that she would and stuck by her side. She slowly regained herself and was improving, but then I became depressed.

To overcome my depression, I studied counseling. It was so inspiring that I realized I wanted to help those in pain as a counselor.

I've come to realize that all of my painful experiences led me to discover my true purpose. And when my brother, who had experienced these same adversities, expressed his confidence in me, that was the final push I needed.

It has been 12 years since I began counseling and I have not forgotten what I've experienced. I work to pay it forward and connect it to the future.

As thanks to God for helping me during that time, I began hosting shrine tours to invite people to get to know shrines more deeply. As in times past, shrines are a place of connection. They bring people together. I produce such events at shrines to help others connect with themselves and others.

Since I was a child, I overcame many adversities, including my mother's mental health, the discord between my parents, and my own depression. But I also experienced many miracles that came out of those devastating situations, and all of my desires have subsequently come true. After all of this, I was married at 38, and though people said it would be difficult to get pregnant naturally, I did and gave birth at 40.

I discovered the Passion Test, and, through that, I remembered what I truly wanted to do, so I held my own seminars and opened the Grace Mind Academy to share my knowledge about living life authentically.

Now, I am set to publish my very first book. I am fulfilled in both my private life and my professional life. My younger brother also got married and now has two children.

These experiences have taught me that no matter what you have gone through or may be going through, there is a reason to have hope. In fact, your adversity may be the very thing that will open up your life's purpose to you. Let me share seven important lessons from my experiences that may be helpful to you.

1. Give thanks and show appreciation to live a life of gratitude

Japanese people consider gratitude to be very important. From ancient times, the Japanese have believed that God is within all elements of nature—even in a single plant—and that we are alive by the grace of nature. In the Shinto religion, it is believed that there is an almost infinite number of spirits that are within the sun, moon, the stars, wind, lightning, land, fields, mountains, rivers, stones, and even in kitchens and bathrooms, as well as in animals and academia. Of course, God is also within humans. This is known as God's divided spirit. And giving thanks is like a prayer to acknowledge that you are alive thanks to all of God's creations.

Even in the worst situations in life, there is always something to be thankful for, if you're willing to look for it. Often our most difficult times are the precursor to our greatest breakthroughs.

My mentor and Japan's number one investor, Wahei Takeda, had this same belief and developed many businesses. When I asked him, "What should I do when I feel low?" he responded with laughter.

"If something bad happens, that means you're not grateful enough. When that happens, you just have to say, 'Thank you' a million times."

Since then, whenever I face issues, I check in with myself to see if I have been showing my appreciation.

And at shrines, rather than asking for something, I express my gratitude. I strive to always say thank you to my ancestors, my parents, and the people around me.

2. Cherish connection: The Japanese art of Wa (harmony)

The Japanese people have valued "Wa (harmony)" from the beginning of time. It is a part of the traditional Japanese spirit, and it's all about finding harmony with different values, different people, positions, and anything that is in relation to us. It's the spirit of a higher dimension. The Japanese spirit is to value the connection between people and sharing our lives with them.

Another part of this is to treasure old things and create something new out of that.

Taking action for yourself while thinking of others—in other words, the act of bringing happiness to others to bring yourself happiness—is one of the teachings of Buddhism.

This very teaching is utilized in business by successful people like Kazuo Inamori, the founder of massive corporations like the Kyocera Group and KDDI, as well as by Konosuke Matsushita, the founder of Panasonic. Many corporations in Japan operate with this in mind.

By purely accepting other people and society and connecting with them, we can create harmony and expand in the best way possible.

3. The importance of fate: how to utilize the gift of fate

Fate is something that happens when the unseen, mystical aspects of life come together to create synchronicity. Everything that happens, everyone you meet, is not because of coincidence but because of necessity. By being mindful of fateful happenings and cherishing the experience, you will experience more synchronicity and more of the blessings of fate.

Ichi-go Ichi-e (a Japanese saying that came out of the art of Sado (tea ceremony) means that the time spent together is a very precious, one-time experience, so we must cherish this time together now as it won't come again.

In Sado, the tea is served with the assumption that you only get to meet someone once so you must serve them to the best of your ability. For my family, we wanted to show our appreciation to the person who bought our house, so we invited him into our home to enjoy a dinner that I made myself.

This concept not only applies to the people that you meet but also to the things around us. When you treat every moment as a special, unique moment that will never come again, it can create a truly wonderful and fateful connection. This will begin a positive cycle that will lead to more connections and expansion.

4. Enjoy the present moment by thinking "everything is going to be okay!" . . . everything is perfect

Since I was a child, I've overcome many difficult experiences. But somehow, deep inside of me, I always thought that "everything is going to be okay!" and "It will get better." So even when people gave up on me or said something was impossible, all my wishes came true.

I believe this was because the innocent belief I held as a child has continued to live in me somewhere deep in my subconscious. I have always said to myself and to my family that "everything is going to be okay!" and "It will get better." And that thought in the present moment appears in the future. Rather than filling up your present with worries, fill it up with the feeling of "It's going to be okay" and enjoy this moment. You are always on the road to perfection.

Buddhism teaches us about the impermanence of this world. Everything is impermanent and continues to evolve. It means that things that don't evolve do not actually exist.

Life is impermanent; therefore, we must live in the moment. Pour all of your energy into the present. If you have any worries, just repeat the words: "everything is going to be okay!" "It will get better."

This will help you change the energy of worry into the energy of fun or joy. Worry is a thing of our past or future, so by repeating these words, you can come back to the present.

I also recommend going to visit a shrine, a temple, or a church. Just by visiting you will be cleansed and feel refreshed. In Japan, we have many shrines, but you can also go to places in nature that help you feel calm, like the ocean, mountains, or lakes, so you can breathe deeply. Fill up your daily life with things that make you feel good like listening to your favorite music, going to see a film, or playing with your children.

5. Do not give up, just believe: The power of belief

Dreams come true when you don't give up. Believe in this vast universe, in God, and, most of all, in yourself. My father was someone who always believed in others, even after being fooled. And because he was like this, so many people showed up to help him when he needed it the most. This is because he built such a deep, trusting relationship with those around him and because he worked so hard for his family and his employees. No matter what the situation, there is always something you can learn from that situation.

People are always growing. Dreams and wishes can become a reality. A future that you can't even imagine awaits you. So please don't give up on your dreams.

Your wishes come true int the very best timing. So do not give up but, instead, do what you can do right now until that time comes. To truly believe is to surrender to the flow of this massive universe. You cannot let go and surrender without trust.

In the past, I would persist in my own thoughts and was stuck on things. But through all of my experiences, I learned that trusting this big universe was the most freeing way to be and that I could reach places I never thought I would. If your wish comes from within your soul, it will definitely come true. So, release all of your inner hopes and wishes and continue to believe in them.

6. Interact with others with thoughtfulness, kindness, and devotion

Connecting with others deeply and harmoniously is one of the keys to happiness. When I was going through a truly difficult time, I was saved over and over by the kind words and actions of others. I will never be able to forget the people who helped us. I'm also grateful for my parents and my younger brother. Now, I'm a mother myself. I hope to teach my child about thoughtfulness and kindness as well.

As my grandparents and parents taught me thoughtfulness and kindness, I believe that my own actions will naturally teach those things to my child.

When it comes to counseling, I make sure I listen closely to understand how the person feels. When we are faced with difficulty, it can be such a relief to just talk about what is happening. If someone is going through something, listening to them, or even just smiling at them can give them a feeling of being heard and accepted.

When you interact with others with the sense of honoring God in them, you can create deep connections with them. When people connect on a deeper level, love flows between them. This is because our true essence is love.

7. Love yourself: A way of knowing your true self

Ever since I was a child, I would make an effort to please the people around me. And when I became depressed at 24, I spent a decade after that reading all kinds of books. I learned how to be honest with myself, how to depend on others, and how to be my authentic self. To love yourself, you must first listen to your inner voice. You must listen for your soul's voice, through the thick shell of your past beliefs and societal conditioning. You must take action based on what your inner voice tells you.

I try to do this over and over, especially when I experience a negative emotion.

Every human is love itself and no two people are the same; we are a precious existence. So, please, take care of yourself first. And by doing that, you'll create a ripple effect of love that helps those around you find happiness.

Learning to love myself was challenging for me. But I learned from every single person I ever met. The challenges helped my love grow deeper and deeper.

Through different experiences, events, and relationships with others, you will able to get to know yourself more completely. If you are filled with emotion, take a moment to have a conversation with yourself. Believe in your inner voice instead of your thoughts and follow your instincts and senses.

Finally, anything that you need, whether it's information, money, or a wish fulfillment, comes to you through other people. So, first, please show your gratitude to the people in front of you. Please cherish each moment of every day by fully living it. Our souls may be eternal, but our lives are finite. Be grateful to have this life and challenge yourself with infinite possibilities because our lives are finite.

These seven lessons have been fundamental to the Japanese people since ancient times, and it's the Japanese way of creating a better fortune.

In Japan, we have seasonal celebrations that celebrate the different seasons of both nature and of human life. From New Year celebrations to the girl's festival in March, as well as the October full moon to the winter solstice, on top of christenings, birthdays, and weddings, these celebrations give us a chance to give thanks to God and ask for continued protection. The Japanese people go to the shrine and to the temple to communicate with our ancestors and ourselves, and even in our daily life, we give thanks before and after meals with our hands together.

I believe that being grateful for the things you cannot see and acknowledging them is the key to experience miracles in your daily life. I now feel that each moment I'm alive is a true miracle and not just those special miracles. There are miracles even in the mundane.

True happiness, success, and abundance is something that comes from within, and by practicing these seven lessons, you will become fulfilled and your dreams and wishes will naturally come true.

Tomomi Tsukiyama was born in Aichi Prefecture, Japan. Today she is the President of the Grace Mind Academy and is a writer, event producer, spiritual counselor, and Asia's #1 connector. Tomomi is a spiritual counselor and in 2006 founded the Healing Salon Qualia in Japan. She has provided support for more than 10,000 people. She is a connector who connects the edges of everything with love. She has spent more than 30 years of research in the spiritual world, gaining knowledge and experience with psychological counseling, learning to heal the wounds of the Japanese heart, exploring the root cause of those who are suffering, discovering her unique talents, and recognizing the value of existence. At the age of 40, she gave birth and dedicated herself to raising her children for 5 years. After returning to the working world, she now organizes spiritually based events and seminars. She has led events with celebrities, bestselling authors, and company heads that have been attended by more than 3,500 people. She guides her clients through the spiritual traditions of Japan, showing them how to increase their luck as they connect with the essence of a shrine. Tomomi is a protege of the late Japanese investor, Wahei Takeda, called by some, "the Warren Buffet of Japan." Her first book was published by Sunmark Publishing in 2020.

Chapter 14

TURNING PERFORMANCE PRESSURE INTO WORKDAY PLEASURE

By Andrea Danner (Germany)

....

Tears were streaming down my face as I sat in bed on yet another Sunday morning. Grey skies outside seemed to reflect the greyness that was covering my soul. How many times have I sat on this bed crying my eyes out while the girls still sleep?

Heavy, pushy thoughts in this world of greyness were invading my mind: "Stop crying! Try harder! Get your act together!"

But I couldn't anymore. My shoulders were sinking with resignation, feeling as if I had to carry all the responsibilities of the world. I felt pressure. Massive pressure. It was like being in a car press. Ruthless and without any hope to get out, the walls were closing in.

My heart was tightening, turning into cold dark stone—no warmth left. I was sobbing even more.

There it was again, all this pressure to make a living, to be a good mom, to be a good daughter and sister, to outperform in my job as a leader, to live up to high standards of excellence, never-ending to-do lists that never got done in time. I was so tired of this!

Next to me was a huge pile of books on western and eastern philosophies, positive thinking, meditation, affirmation, compassion, how to let go, and much more. Right in front of me was my computer, with tons of self-help programs that I had started to take since my second divorce. I must have spent thousands of dollars by now. With only baby step results.

With a sudden rush I saw pictures of myself. Situations I had lived through over the last 2 years. Me coming home tired, reacting with exhaustion. Frustrated that my girls were not performing to my self-imposed standards. Taking it out on them because I wasn't either.

There was no more laughter in our home. I could hardly stand listening to music. Time with my girls was focused on duty. Time for me didn't exist. I felt such an ocean deep sadness, that I have been hiding for so long. I saw myself being overwhelmed and overworked—I was sinking into the ground. I had been giving more than I had, relentlessly with no mercy. Working hard on being excellent—trying to be perfect. Working long hours, driving myself, never getting anywhere. I was so done with that.

I've come to realize that I wasn't alone. Did you know that only 13 percent of employees worldwide are engaged (Gallup Study on worldwide Employee Engagement 2017)? And that a recent study at the Yale Center for Emotional Intelligence pointed out that 1 out of 5 engaged employees are running the risk of burnout? The survey examined the levels of engagement and burnout in more than 1,000 U.S. employees. They found that for some people engagement is indeed a purely positive experience; after all, 2 out of 5 employees reported high engagement and low burnout.

"However increasing pressure, setting higher goals and tighter timelines, developing more projects, changing the organization or the leadership style to more agility and other latest trends is just creating the opposite of what was intended" (HBR, Feb. 2018, 1 in 5 Highly Engaged Employees at Risk of Burnout).

It is not just about engagement or ambition, but it is engagement with meaning, ease, and positive outcomes that lead to work that is fulfilling . . . as I was about to discover.

This morning was about to change my life—not overnight, but slowly and surely, certainly visible for everyone in the course of the next year.

As always on these Sunday mornings, I started searching the internet for some solace. And this morning I stumbled onto a video with Janet Bray Attwood. She'd created something called The Passion Test. And she was talking about living a passionate life. I knew immediately: THAT WAS IT!

Passion, laughter, a loving warmth was coming across from Janet via my screen. I felt relief—the press stopped. I felt ease and the weight on my shoulders lifting—slowly, but steadily, I felt the sun coming through the veil of grey that covered my soul. Janet was spreading such an atmosphere of passionate lovingness that I immediately felt a warm, bright light coming into my heart.

That's what I was missing—PASSION! I didn't have any passion left in my body. Let alone any light-heartedness.

I was running on empty batteries, squeezing out the last energy to go through my day. I wanted and needed to have what Janet had. Living a passionate life, getting up in the morning with ease, looking forward to doing what I am here for in this world and enjoying the ride. And that moment I decided I would do everything that is necessary to change my life for the better. This was in April 2017 and it took me a year to really follow that path with rigor, develop trust to leave my life of pressure, and experience pleasure—almost every day.

I became a certified Passion Test facilitator that April and found my core and work passions later that year. I started to feel lighter and got more energy every day. And I started to work on my passion to "Inspire leaders to create engagement leading from their heart." Being a catalyst in times of change, supporting leaders to engage their teams through pleasure instead of pressure, is what gets me up in the morning, is keeping me energized throughout the day, and just fills my heart.

Inspired by this wonderful journey to discover my passions, my signature program was born: The A-R-T of Performance – From Pressure to Pleasure! We successfully launched the first pilot in 2017 and are now getting ready for the next phase of wonderful training processes—supporting leaders and their teams to live a work life of pleasure in a challenging, ever-changing, high-speed world.

My energy is mostly high these days. I have so much more fun in what I'm doing, my income is increasing steadily, and I have this incredible feeling that being a change catalyst for leaders is just what I am here to be. And it all began with finding my passions!

The Leadership Challenge in a Fast-Changing and Challenging World

Due to high pressure and—as a consequence—increasing burnout, companies, as well as our healthcare and social systems, are facing costs in the multiple billions of dollars. And, more importantly, it costs the lives of individuals—mothers, fathers, friends, neighbors, or coworkers. It costs their freedom, their joy and happiness, and the energy to feeling alive and fulfilled. A birthright that we have given up.

By now everyone knows a person who faces burnout or is actively disengaged, actually consciously or unconsciously undermining their company rather than contributing to its success. Leaders in companies try to do all kinds of things to get the performance so necessary to increase profits, market share, or even to stay in the market. However, it seems that they fail spectacularly. Not on purpose. Unconsciously—without understanding the dynamics of merging head and heart to move from pressure to pleasure.

With more than 27 years of experience and expertise in leadership roles, as a coach and consultant, for me, living a fulfilled and balanced life as a leader boils down to understanding and following three steps:

1. **A—Acknowledge: Understand yourself and get clarity on your direction.** Getting to know your inner drivers, competencies, challenges and blind spots; knowing your purpose, your passions and finding the theme that is driving you as a leader, beyond your daily tasks and routine. Get inspiration that lasts!

2. **R—Release Potential: Break the glass ceiling and tap into your full power.** Understand what is keeping you back—every day—from being your best, with ease. Understand the mental patterns that are your glass ceiling. Understand your set of values and beliefs that keeps you in your loop, holding you back from living a fulfilled live as a leader. Find ways to remove stuckness any time you experience it and get into your utmost power to grow and thrive the way you want. Create a continuous process of feeling empowered and fulfilled.

3. **T—Take charge: Create a fulfilled live through self-love and daily actions.** Self-compassion, become your best friend/ lover, care for you first, find a set of rituals that provides the structure for change in an easy way. Connect with your higher power regularly to stay on track.

Let's now put those principles into practice:

Step 1—Acknowledge
Exercise 1: What for?

Before moving to passions and purpose, ask the question "For what am I doing what I am currently doing?"

1. Make sure to have a pencil and paper ready. Yes, the old way!
2. Take at least 10 minutes. Get out everything that comes to your mind. And when you feel empty, just sit and wait a little longer. This way you are tapping into your subconscious mind for deeper insights.

Step 2—Release potential
Exercise 2: What's holding me back?

Often our beliefs are neatly linked to deep-seated values. While we may not go deep here, a first inquiry may be: "What do I want to be doing and why am I not doing what I want to be doing? What could be a conflicting belief?" Please use the above process to reflect on the questions below:

a. What should I be doing—what is my visible commitment to me/others? For example: I should be leading by example.

b. What am I doing/not doing instead? For example: I'm waiting for someone else to tell me what the priorities are.

c. What could be a hidden competing commitment? For example: Seeking others' approval.

Step 3—Take charge
Exercise 3: What little step could I take that feels secure and easy?

Very often we postpone change because the change feels so big and overwhelming. What is an easy step you could take, each day, to get you started in a good direction? Rome was not conquered overnight. Change needs time and ease to perform the change. Please use the above process to reflect on the questions below:

1. What is an easy, enjoyable thing that I could do—every day—that would make my life easier/more enjoyable? Examples: Start the day with the following:

   • Have a short reflection on what you are grateful for to start the day with good energy.

- Take some time to reflect on the three things you want to accomplish today (and why).
- Think about what does not serve you this day and what you can leave out!

2. Then ask the questions:
   - Who/what could hinder me in doing that?
   - Who/what could support me in doing that?
   - What will be the benefit?

These little exercises will get you on your way. These are the first steps to acknowledge what is already there—based on your expertise, experience, and just knowing. Only to the degree you are aware are you able to change. Please use this awareness to start your own path from pressure to pleasure.

From my personal perspective and experience, only leaders who are connected to their passions and purpose, who understand their inner driving forces and know how to release resistance to get to their full potential, only leaders who are living their passions full out can provide the inspiration, empowerment, and connection that is necessary to lead in this fast-moving world of growing uncertainty and individual pain.

Only to the extent that leaders have clarity and tools to release potential will they be able to inspire and empower their teams to perform at a top level with ease and engagement. Only to the extent that they are connected to themselves will they be able to connect to their team, building an energetic basis to move in one direction—effortlessly and almost guided by an invisible force.

And whether you're leading a team, or a family, or your own life, these same principles can help you to step up to a new level of happiness and contribution.

Andrea Danner is the owner of AD Leadership Consulting GmbH in Hamburg, Germany. Throughout the last 27 years she has successfully worked with leaders of international companies in the area of selection and development, either as a principal consultant in international consultancies or as senior HR Executive, being part of management teams, such as Pepsi Cola Germany. Her driving force is to create clarity and provide guidance for leaders and their teams to perform at high levels of excellence with passion and ease instead of pressure and pain. Contact Andrea Danner at anfrage@ad-leadership.de.

Chapter 15
FROM HEARTBREAK TO HAPPINESS

By Akiko Kaneko (Japan)

....

As I opened my eyes, I saw a white ceiling above me. For a moment, I wondered where I was, but then realized that I was in a hospital bed.

"Oh, it's done." As soon as that thought occurred, emptiness took over me.

"There is no one in my belly anymore." My whole body felt like it had been emptied out.

"What have I done?!" A sense of worthlessness began to attack me.

I thought it would be okay. I wanted to properly parent my older two children, but this feeling was not what I wanted.

I felt my instincts kick in.

I could never tell my daughter or my son what had happened. I could never tell them that I took their sibling's life. I thought to myself, "I will keep this buried inside me and take it to my grave."

But the horror of what I'd done continued to haunt me. Even if I hadn't told anyone, *I* knew.

"You took your own child's life."

"You're not worthy of being a teacher."

"What a terrible human being."

I threw those words at myself again and again.

It became so painful that my husband and I went all the way to Aomori to the sacred mountain of Osore-zan. We stopped at the memorial for aborted and miscarried fetuses to pray.

But when I was busy, concentrating on work, it felt as though I could forget about it all, so I poured myself into my job. No matter what school I worked at, there were difficulties, but it was rewarding, and it gave me new challenges to face.

In this chapter, I will take you on my journey and, before we're done, I'll share the lessons that transformed my life into the life of true joy it is today. If there's any part of your life about which you feel ashamed, that you regret, or where you feel you made an irrevocable mistake, my hope is that my story and lessons will help you to use that experience to bring you to a new level of fulfillment in your own life.

How It All Began

The first school I worked at was in Muramatsu, at Kawauchi Elementary School. For the first time, I watched kids run around their desks and thought, "Wow, I didn't know elementary school kids run around like this!" As a brand-new teacher, each day was filled with surprises.

On Sundays, I went to the river with my kids—jumping off rocks and swimming in the deep water. When midges would fly at us, we'd yell "duck!" and watch the bugs fly in circles from beneath the surface of the water. We'd have a bonfire nearby and buried potatoes in it, so after swimming for a couple of hours, we'd find deliciously cooked potatoes in the fire and eat them as our snacks. What I know about nature was taught by my students.

Being a Working Mother of Two Children

I met my husband and married him as I transferred to another school. During my time at this school, I either had a baby in my belly or I was on parental leave, but whenever I would visit homes for a parent–teacher conference, my students would follow me from the first home to the very last one. I felt adored.

When I had morning sickness, I would have to drive around with a plastic bag in one hand. When I got home, I was so tired I'd fall asleep straight away.

The next school I worked at was a large school with 5 teachers per grade, and I was very excited as they asked me to head up the assembly committee. I would put on educational plays that were enjoyed by the whole school, where the storyline was about saving children who were kidnapped by an evil character. We even put on a Disney Parade around the school by hooking up a two-wheeled cart to my car.

It was a fun, exciting time, filled with challenges, and with achievements.

Building a Career and Finding Fulfilment . . . and Busyness

At the next school I worked for, I not only looked after my own class, but I was also the head of research. We would go look for ruins of old castles on mountains, we re-created a Jomon-era dwelling and made clay pottery or dug up fossils. I also took on the role of the head of environment, where I organized pairs of one student and one elder of the community. The student would grow two potted plants, one for themselves and the other for the elder. I can never forget the letters of appreciation sent from those elders, written with shaky hands. That was over 20 years ago, but to know that program is still in place brings me great joy.

Becoming Pregnant with a Third Child

At the next school, for the first time, I did not have my own class. I was the head of training. When I first arrived at the school, the job was hard for me as I was met with resistance. One teacher was even asking why they had to be involved.

I was so relieved three years later when that very teacher said they were glad to have done the training. During this time, I taught math to every grade. I taught students who refused to come to school, and I even taught math to massive classes of 50–60 students at one time. Every day was challenging, but these times were also fulfilling because I was able to overcome the challenges.

It was then that I discovered I had become pregnant with my third child.

Back then, every morning I would drop one child off at the daycare as it opened, then rush to take the other to kindergarten. I couldn't possibly raise another child. I wanted to work. I loved my work and it gave me great fulfillment. It also paid the bills. And that's how I made the regrettable choice to have an abortion.

I began questioning why I was born and what happiness meant to me. Both my teaching career and raising my children were very important. I could never have chosen one or the other, but I made a choice in favor of one and that led me to make a mistake I could not take back.

The Vice Principal I Hated and Making Life-Changing Decisions

On top of everything else at this time, a young vice principal was transferred to my school and we clashed. It started with her changing the training day I held for newly hired teachers. I was working so hard and I felt I couldn't forgive such a thing, so I told her how I felt. She said to me, "I don't even want to see your face," but I persisted because I had something to say. I'm sure it was uncomfortable for her.

Without asking me, this same vice principal enrolled me into a study group for vice principal candidates. That did not go down well with me; I didn't understand why I had to study, and I continued to think very negatively about this whole situation.

Then one day, I was called in by the principal. "If you really don't want to do it, you can quit," he said, and, in that moment, I wondered what I really wanted to do. I became a teacher because I loved children. I enjoyed my work and I didn't become a teacher to become a principal. It couldn't possibly be fun to be told what to do by other people. So how can I do what I really want to do? But then I thought, maybe by being a principal I can bring happiness to many more students. So, after much consideration, I decided to study and applied myself to it for a whole year. Somehow, that resulted in my being selected to become a vice principal.

Becoming a Vice Principal

At my very first school as a vice principal, I looked after a mammoth-sized school of over 1,000 students. On top of that, the school was in the midst of renovating the very old school building. There were 80 teachers at the school, and I was beyond busy.

However, having so many teachers depending on me, my work felt very satisfying and rewarding. I actively paid attention to any troubles and helped resolve them. With so many people, we created a system where any problem that arose was written into a notebook. Within 3 years, we had over 20 notebooks. And all of them got resolved.

To take care of the renovations, I put on a helmet and met with construction workers, making decisions on everything, all the way down to the color of the curtains. With the help of a supplier, I even developed my own vacuum machine, which was like a large blackboard eraser that had a large suctioning mop. Every day was full of excitement.

Once the renovations were completed, we threw a celebratory completion ceremony. There I watched 1,000 people move their bodies to music and enjoy themselves as they watched a choir made up of our students, community members, and teachers singing along to the music played by people of Nagaoka Symphony. I was moved, proud of the hard work I put in and what it had accomplished.

Advice from My Principal

The first school I looked after as a principal was Naigo Elementary School in Kashiwazaki city. The work was so different from that of a vice principal, and I felt confused in the beginning. I wasn't directly involved with the teaching at the school and had very little contact with the students, so I wasn't sure what to do. That's when a more senior female school principal said to me, "If you're going to do it, you may as well do your best at what you want to do. Otherwise it's a waste."

With this advice, I was inspired. I realized that it would be boring if I didn't do what I hoped to do as a principal, so I decided to challenge myself. At this school, I developed a program where together with community members, our students would go to maintain the mountain that stood behind the school. I also connected our students with a local theatre group to put on plays. This project was titled the "Nishiyama Happy Project." It brought together other local schools and high schools, as well as choirs and dance teams in collaboration, and brought vitality back to Nishiyama. I can't express how happy it makes me that this project is still going, even after my departure.

Finding Friends Outside of the School

I began to feel how lonely it is to be a principal. I felt sadness at not being able to have a laugh and be with students every day like teachers did. It was then that I saw a sign that jumped out in front of me, "Would you like to make life-long friends?" This was an advertisement for a trainer's camp named Tentsuku-man and it was being held in Niigata, not far from where I lived.

So, I decided to join. As soon as I arrived, I was met by people who spoke with honesty, and I cried a lot during those days. At the end of the three days, I stood under a waterfall and yelled out, "I am going to create the smiliest school in Japan!"

To this day, I remain close friends with the 25 attendees who came from all over Japan. I am very grateful for them. I watch Tentsuku-man take on challenges all the time. He is one of my mentors.

My other mentor is Kotaro Hisui. He has written many bestsellers in Japan, yet he treats everyone fairly and I truly respect him. I got to join his "Hisui Academy" and "Hisui Lab," where I have met many of my dear friends. Together we put on the Rainbow Festival and have taken part in fashion shows as well.

Encountering Passion

I came to learn from Janet Bray Attwood in a way that surprised me. I had taken Janet's course to become a Passion Test facilitator. The course was so powerful and I learned so much that when my friend signed up to go to Italy to learn from Janet, I decided to go as well. Janet is truly a passionate person who sees deeply into the hearts of her students. She really understood us very well and accepted the challenges as if they were her own.

In Italy, a lot of things that had tormented me bubbled up and, for a short time, I felt unstable. However, thanks to Janet's love and guidance, I learned to love myself despite all of that. I came to realize that self-love is the basis and foundation of all growth and progress in life.

Living My Passions

My challenges as a school principal still continue to this day. But now, I only do what is true to myself and what makes me feel excited.

One of my latest endeavors is running a "Parenting Advice Meeting" at Katagai Elementary School with Miki Itakura to help parents clear their worries. I also started a "Gathering of Happiness" to support the mental health of teachers. We spend 30 minutes doing an exercise to feel happy, then we all eat my homemade dinner together. It has brought us all together, so we feel so much closer.

I've also taken on being a part of musicals, which was a childhood dream. These activities fit in with a few of my top five passions. My number-one passion is to create an exciting space with someone I love, number two is to shine bright and be healthy while I challenge myself with exciting things, and number four is to see people enjoy my cooking.

Once I began living my passions and people came to know that I teach the Passion Test, someone asked me if she could take the Passion Test with me. She came to my home and while we were going through it, a traumatized child self of her past came out. She was in tears wanting to reject her past self. So, I held her and helped her heal her past self. This experience allowed me to realize that I also was living my other passion, to share how to live an exciting life with others, and my fifth passion, to work with people who've found their passion to change the world. My top five passions have all come true.

Keys to Living an Authentic Life

From all these experiences, I've learned lessons that have brought me great fulfillment, and that's what I want for you. So, let me share with you what I've discovered are the keys to living a fulfilled life:

1. Face your heart and ask what it really wants to do.
2. Always choose the exciting option when making life-changing decisions.

3. Find your top 5 passions and live your own passions.

4. Value and focus on what excites you about working.

5. Find a mentor. If you find someone who is happy and doing what they truly want to do, spend some time with them and imitate them.

6. Find people you can connect with and help each other make your dreams come true.

7. Use as much of the 24 hours of the day as possible for your passions. Be prepared to let other things go.

8. Find friends who can help you gain a new level of perspective.

9. Take initiative as the main character of your own life.

Life can be a miracle when you choose it to be. I hope you will take these lessons and make your own life a miracle for yourself and those around you.

Akiko Kaneko *was born in Nagaoka City in the Niigata Prefecture of Japan. After graduating from Niigata University with a degree in education, Akiko followed her love of children to become an elementary school teacher. Serving as a teacher for 37 years, she had the opportunity to become a vice principal and then a principal in Japan. Although she resisted making the switch from being a teacher to becoming an administrator, she realized she could impact the lives of even more children as a school principal. Out of her pursuit of what an authentic education is, Akiko has participated in the seminars of Tensekuman (a famous Japanese "edutainer") and Hisakotaro (a famous bestselling author and speaker). She challenges herself to experience new things through fashion shows, musicals, and a film production, all with the goal to raise happy children who smile.*

Chapter 16
LIKE A PHOENIX

By Tou Suppunabul (Thailand)

· ·

I was lying in bed in a dark, quiet room in the middle of the night. My eyes were wide open as I reflected on my life—my dull, empty life. I looked around seeing only the darkness and hearing only the sound of my heavy sighs.

"I don't want to be alive," I thought.

I couldn't lie still. I felt intense pain in my stomach as if someone was squeezing my colon. I bent my knees, moving them toward my chest with my hands pressed against my stomach to relieve the pain, but it didn't help. It just got worse until tears started streaming down my face.

I let my body suffer that pain without taking any pills or running to a doctor. Perhaps it was my way of torturing myself, adding more pressure to my life. The pain lasted for hours and only faded a little before dawn.

The morning came and my boring, senseless, mundane life continued. Riding a crowded train with barely enough room for me to stand, I arrived an hour later at the modern office building in downtown Bangkok where I worked. My head felt heavy with tension in my neck and shoulders as I walked into the newsroom where I had been working for about eight years as a business journalist.

I turned on the two, 17-inch computer screens I used to monitor the news feed. Part of my job was to file a headline as soon as I saw important information. The news feed scrolled non-stop and my eyes stared at the screen.

This was the day when companies listed on the Thai stock exchange filed their financial statements. That meant the pressure on me ratcheted up. I had to keep an eye on the screen without blinking to be sure I didn't miss anything, as the information flew in, non-stop, line by line.

Once I spotted an important piece of news, I sent the headline to my editors as soon as I could, so business news subscribers could get up-to-date information for their investment decisions. If I failed to file timely stories on important news events, it meant I'd have to explain myself to my supervisor. I avoided such embarrassment at all costs.

On this day, as I watched the screen, I felt bored—fed up with working under time pressure and having to compete with other news agencies in a matter of seconds.

Being the first in reporting a story, yet maintaining the accuracy of the story, used to be a fun, exciting challenge for me. Earlier in my career, I attended a media briefing by the Thai prime minister where dozens of reporters gathered around, asking questions. I had to get a spot close to him to be able to ask questions, hear his answers, and take notes. Soon after the press conference was over, I called in the story right away. Yet, it turned out that my story was a few seconds behind another news organization. My editor called me into his office and insisted that I explain why I lost to our competitors.

The loss upset me and put more pressure on me to beat competitors the next time. Having worked for news agencies for over a decade doing this competitive and time-pressured job, the stress had been building in me day by day. As the stress intensified, I lost my passion for this work that had once been my dream job. I became like a robot, doing only what was required of me. My happiness and enthusiasm at work had faded, leaving me with insomnia and stress-induced gastritis.

I dreamed of being a reporter as long as I can remember. My dad owned a local newspaper and I loved the idea of sharing messages that benefit people. I was proud of working at this prestigious news organization where I had opportunities to interview people from all walks of life, from the prime minister, top executives of multinational companies, and entrepreneurs, all the way to local farmers.

As I lay in bed clutching my stomach in bed that night, I was at the high point of my career. I covered events both in Thailand and other Southeast Asian countries. I earned an impressive income compared with peers my age, but my mind and heart felt empty, distressed, devoid of happiness. I kept wondering, how could it be that I hated what was once my dream job?

Then one day, I attended a seminar on finding life purpose and passion. It was like a wake-up call for me. As I sat in the workshop, I realized it was time for me to leave worry behind, to reframe my past stressful experiences with empowering new perspectives and learn to enjoy every moment in life.

I found that my past failures and stress made me feel that I wasn't good enough. I beat myself up repeatedly in my mind, blaming myself when I couldn't accomplish the tasks required of me to the level of quality I expected of myself, or when I couldn't win against competitors in my field of work.

From what I learned in that seminar, I let go of worry and stress while embracing gratitude about the things I have in life that are wonderful. I started to appreciate the job I have, all my belongings, the money I made, and the friends around me. I learned to appreciate and celebrate my past success, awarding myself a trophy for my accomplishments, both big and small.

Expressing gratitude and celebrating your success seems so simple, yet it's so powerful. If you are struggling in your own job, these are the first practices to begin. I encourage you to make them part of your daily routine.

Here's what I do . . . As I wake up in the morning, the first thing I do is express gratitude to my body, my life, the things I have, and the people in my life who love and appreciate me. When I'm in bed at night, I express gratitude again for the good that happened to me that day. Every time I finish an assignment or accomplish what I've planned, I pat my chest a few times and say, "You're awesome."

The more I appreciate what I have, the more happiness grows in my life. I smile more often, have more energy at work. I no longer have problems sleeping nor do I suffer from stomach pain through the night.

That seminar also triggered an important question that we each need to ask ourselves: "What do I want to do for the rest of my life that will make me happy and fulfilled?" I pondered this question and felt that I want to be a "life coach" as I want to facilitate others to live happily, showing others how to leave their worries behind and creating a positive conclusion in every situation of their lives.

I decided to pursue a path to become a certified coach.

It was the evening after a full day of learning. About 300 people gathered in a field in a half-circle. We watched our teacher light stacks of wood on fire that were set in three different lanes.

Standing there watching the flames with my friends, I got energized and inspired to stay determined to make my dream come true, no matter what obstacles I may have along the way. As the wood burned, our teacher explained that we would each walk across the hot coals left by those flames.

My friends and I practiced skills that helped us focus on achieving our goals and accomplishing this fire walk safely. As part of the practice, I walked barefoot on the ground dozens of times, repeating the goal statement I'd written to help me stay focused on what I wanted to achieve.

The moment of my test arrived. I stood right in front of the burning, red coals, hearing the crackling sounds of the wood burning and feeling the heat from the fire. Fear popped up. I adjusted my posture, standing with confidence, and said my goal out loud: "I am a world-class coach and trainer who serves people to live passionately with fulfillment."

My eyes focused on the end of the lane where my teacher stood, about 3 meters away. Then I started to take my first step, walking on those hot coals. Surprisingly, I didn't feel any heat. I kept walking step by step firmly and slowly until the end of the lane. When I got to the other end, I screamed with joy, celebrating my success in achieving this amazing task.

This was an unbelievable moment for me. I couldn't believe that my feet didn't get burned, nor did I feel any heat when I walked on the coals. It made me realize the power we each hold in our minds. Your thoughts can empower you or destroy you . . . it's your choice. Walking on those coals was something I never thought I could do. By doing it, my beliefs about what's possible expanded, just as what's possible can expand for you when you allow yourself to step into the fire of your own discomfort.

As I continued to work full-time as a reporter, I spent over a thousand hours learning and practicing coaching skills, until finally I was certified as a master coach of Neuro-Linguistic Programming.

As you begin to follow your own heart, to step out of your comfort zone into a field of new possibilities, new opportunities will start to arise when you least expect them.

One day I was surfing on Facebook, looking for interesting content, when I ran across an advertisement. A picture stared out at me of a beautiful, red-headed American woman. The ad said, "Create Your Fabulous Life."

I clicked on the link, and it took me to a page describing a three-hour seminar to discover your passions with this same American woman. "Discover my passions, getting clear on what I love and care about. Hmmm, that sounds interesting!"

I signed up for the seminar and my life got transformed once again. The red-headed, American woman was Janet Bray Attwood, creator of The Passion Test. As I sat in the workshop, did the exercises, and discovered my top 5 passions, I learned the secret that can guarantee anyone a passionate life: "Whenever you're faced with a choice, a decision, or an opportunity, choose in favor of your passions."

The Passion Test process allowed me to open my heart, connect to my feelings, and explore what I truly love and what is meaningful in my life. None of us were ever taught this in school. Neither my teachers nor my parents ever showed me how to express love for myself.

After that event, I came home, looked at myself in the mirror, looked deep into the eyes of the woman I saw, and said: "I love you and accept you for who you are, the way you are. You're a precious and unique gift in this world."

Being mindful and having vibrant, perfect health were my top two passions when I first did the Passion Test process. It was a wake-up call for me. "Self-care" was suddenly a priority. Setting aside time to nurture my mind and body was now part of my "work." I began to take time to exercise, to take care of my physical body. With my new rituals for my body and mind, I lost 30 pounds in three months. I felt more energetic, blissful, and peaceful in every moment.

I began to start the day with meditation and exercise, giving myself time for study, coaching, and doing the Passion Test process, both in groups and with individuals. Seeing people smile, some even with tears in their eyes when they find their top passions, delights me.

I've realized my purpose in life—to help people transform through The Passion Test, the process that allows you to connect to your heart, to your true self, and to live in the flow of nature, in a loving way.

I decided to leave my full-time job to pursue this mission. My goal: to help Thai people live happily aligned with their passions.

It was a scary moment, leaving my secure job with its nice comfortable salary to live in an unknown world, yet one full of possibility. Talking with my boss about my resignation, I felt my heart pounding as I made this big decision, a step that set me free to follow my passions, determine my own destiny, and live a life of adventure rather than boredom. I feel like I am a phoenix that has been reborn to live a new life full of passion, determination, and excitement.

But don't think jumping off the cliff is easy.

My new life changed from being packed into a crowded train every morning and doing long hours of stressful work. Now it begins with getting fresh air in a garden in the morning with mindful exercise and during the day doing the Passion Test and coaching for other people. The more I take people through the Passion Test process, the more I feel confident that I'm walking on the right path, the one on which I feel joyful and am able to contribute to others.

With the clarity of my mission that I gained from the Passion Test, I got a magical opportunity to lead the team organizing an event for Janet Attwood in Thailand. The event was held in a big ballroom at a hotel in Bangkok with an audience of 200 people who learned the importance of self-love. I felt overwhelmed with happiness seeing the attendees smiling and holding one another. "This is what I live my life for," I thought to myself.

Looking back, I see my life unfolding in a way that aligns with my passion and my dreams. It makes me realize my free will creates the life I desire. From a stressful, unhappy person, I have become a blissful person who lives with purpose and passion.

There are some lessons I've learned along the way that may help you live your own passionate life. My recipe:

- Be grateful for what you have and who you are.
- Gain clarity about what you love.
- Have empowering beliefs.
- Trust in the laws of nature.
- Take action passionately.

1. Gratitude is key to creating a relaxed state of mind. I regularly start and end my day by expressing gratitude for what I have to people around me and for situations that happen in my life, both good and challenging ones. When I can find how my challenges have helped me grow and progress, then they become things to be truly grateful for. Expressing gratitude connects me with the feeling of abundance I have in my life.

2. Discovering clarity about what you love through The Passion Test opens the door to a whole new world of possibilities. When I found what I love and followed my passions, it gave me energy to take action relentlessly without getting tired or bored. I go out coaching joyfully without thinking about the financial rewards. When you open your heart to discover what you love and follow your heart's guidance, you discover the source of your own life force.

3. When you investigate the beliefs that have kept you unhappy and replace them with new, empowering beliefs, life will never be the same again. The Work of Byron Katie (www.thework. com) provides a simple yet powerful way to investigate the concepts and beliefs that have kept you miserable so they no longer grip you. Then make a list of those thoughts that support you in living your passions. Say them out loud repeatedly, and you'll begin to gain confidence in your direction. And if you write down a thought like, "I'm living an abundant life," but your mind says "No, you're not," then trying turning the statement into a question. "I'm living an abundant life" becomes "What abundance am I already enjoying in my life?" Your mind will search for the answer to the question and you'll begin to appreciate all the abundance you already enjoy.

4. Trusting in the laws of nature means realizing, deep inside, that life is designed for your benefit. When you adopt this attitude everything changes. In *Happy for No Reason*, the *New York Times* bestseller by Marci Shimoff, the author interviewed over 100 people who others said seemed happy most of the time. Their secret? They found some good, something they could learn from in every situation in their life, even those things others would call "bad." Life is here to help you to know yourself if you're just open to receive the gifts life is giving you.

5. In *The Passion Test* book, it says, "Action engages attention." That means that by taking action you focus your attention on the fulfillment of your desires. Once you know your passions, try creating a plan for the next six months, the

next four weeks, and the next seven days. Each day take a few minutes to plan the next day in advance. Set intentions for the activities you want to achieve the next day that are aligned with your passions. When the new day comes, you're then ready to take powerful action.

I now live a passionate life in a beautiful state, embracing and appreciating every moment. The path isn't paved with rose petals. The road is bumpy sometimes. Yet, my mind feels peaceful and fulfilled. It is like I'm living in heaven every moment, with freedom in my life, knowing that I stand for who I truly am . . . the Phoenix, the passion energizer.

Who will you be? What will you become? You can be, do, and become anything your heart truly desires. First, you need clarity about what that is, then I hope you'll use the steps I've offered to create your own heaven in every moment.

Tou Suppunabul has 20 years' experience as a journalist and communications executive. During her years as a business journalist she interviewed over a thousand people from farmers to Prime Ministers to CEOs of Fortune 500 companies to members of Forbes' list of billionaires. Since 2016, she has dedicated her life to inner work, self-development, coaching, and training. She has helped more than 500 people gain clarity about their passions and have more self-confidence. She also works with teenagers in detention centers to learn self-love. Tou is a national director for The Passion Test in Thailand and also Master Trainer in training for The Passion Test and Mastery of Self Love. Tou is also an interpreter for international speakers who visit Thailand, including New York Times *bestselling authors, Janet Bray Attwood and Chris Attwood, Hollywood director, Larry Gilman, and others. She can be reached at tutoo74@ gmail.com.*

Chapter 17

FROM RED INK TO CLEAR SAILING

By Emi Edwards (Japan)

....

W e both looked down at the toilet. The water looked like melted red ink in a bucket. I saw light reflecting on the rippling water. "I've got blood in my urine," my husband said.

I was in shock, yet I believed with all my heart that my husband would be healthy again because I had the same symptoms long ago, around the time my father passed away in 2011. The stress and upset of his passing resulted in red ink in my toilet as well.

Little did I know that I was entering the busiest and most difficult time in my life.

I met my American husband for the first time in 2005.

I had studied English at university because I loved the language and I wanted to teach Japanese children this language. I knew that if they could speak English many doors would open for them that would otherwise be unavailable.

One day, my English teacher said to me, "There's someone I think you'll enjoy meeting." Intrigued, I agreed to meet this mysterious stranger. My teacher arranged a blind date at a local bar called "Cheers." I wasn't in the habit of going to bars, and to meet a man for the first time? I was nervous. Some young people played pool, others watched the basketball game on the TVs. I didn't see any of it.

When the man who would become my husband walked into the bar that day, I was surprised and a little uncertain. Here was an American man, dressed in the traditional brown kimono worn by philosophers and sages in my country. I thought, "Who is this person?"

As we talked, I learned that he was a professional musician. He'd obtained an artist visa to come from Los Angeles to teach drumming in Tokyo. "Can you make a living doing that?" I asked. I had never thought it was possible for an artist to support themselves, but as it turned out, I was wrong. He was making a very good living.

This has been the story of our relationship. My dear husband makes me think. He opens up new worlds to me. As we talked on that first date, I felt as if I was talking with another me. We both love music. I play the piano. He plays the drums. Neither of us is drawn to competitive sports. And we both have an affinity for philosophy.

My husband loves to read, especially philosophical books. There have been many times when he helps me think differently about my life and, as a result, helps me return to living a happy life.

I remember, years after our first meeting, I was really worried about my job. I worked at Yamaha Music Japan as an English instructor. My income was based on commissions and if I lost students, I lost income. I had no idea if I was doing well or poorly. I worried about money. Even when I wasn't working, I felt fear and terror. It was a very difficult time.

One evening, my husband and I were walking under the moonlight along the Shinano River, Japan's longest river. My husband knew how upset I was and how challenging my work felt. As we walked, he pointed to a ferry and asked, "How does the boat move forward?"

When I said nothing, he asked, "Do you think it's the trails behind it that are pushing it forward?

When I still was quiet, he said, "Or is there a motor that is moving the ferry forward?"

I said, "The motor moves it."

He turned and faced me as he said, "That's right. The motor moves the boat. But if you didn't know anything about the motor, you might think that the trails are pushing it forward."

He continued, "Life is often compared to a river. When the flow of the river is fast, you might try to resist and slow it down. Or when it is flowing slowly you might try to run fast to move it forward more quickly. If you didn't know how the river flows, you might get scared when you are caught in the current.

"But you have a mind, like the motor in the ferry, so you can choose whether to go fast or slow, to go this way or that. When you understand this, then there's no longer anything to be afraid of."

I loved this simple wisdom and it brought peace to my heart.

But now this adorable man who has enriched my life in so many ways has red ink in his toilet. What was I to do? I pulled out all the stops and did everything I could think of to help him.

First, he went to a local clinic. Fortunately, the doctor there spoke English, so I didn't need to take off work to go with him. When I talked to the doctor by phone after my husband's exam, the doctor said, "He needs to go to the prefectural hospital for a more thorough examination. They have the latest technology."

My husband speaks no Japanese, so every time he went to the hospital, I had to come along as his interpreter. Fortunately, I was working as a freelance English teacher which allowed me some flexibility in my schedule. Not so fortunately, my work was in a rural area, two hours' drive from our home. My work started at 3 p.m. each day, so I had to leave by 1 p.m. This made scheduling my husband's medical exams and treatments a challenge. My time schedule was extremely tight.

So almost every day, I'd take my husband to the hospital in the morning, then bring him home, make lunch, then rush off on my two-hour drive to work. I'd work until late in the evening, drive two hours home, and then repeat the whole thing the next day.

It was exhausting.

Fortunately, my mother lived halfway to my work, so sometimes I would stop and rest or stay overnight with her when I could.

In the beginning, the doctors did tests, but they couldn't give us a detailed answer of what was wrong with my husband. Their answers to our questions were vague and we felt frustrated. Finally, the doctor said, "Your husband is going to have to stay at the hospital for three to four days so we can do a biopsy. This is the only way we can know for sure what his ailment is."

The day before the biopsy was scheduled, I got a call from the hospital. "You will need to interpret for your husband in the operating room and while he's in the hospital." So, I quickly arranged my schedule with my work so I could be there for him.

On the day of the biopsy, as I stood in the operating room, dressed in white scrubs, with a mask over my mouth, feeling very out of place, a nurse came in carrying a very heavy x-ray machine, all by herself. Suddenly, she lost her balance and fell into me with this huge machine. I was almost crushed. The doctor was holding his sharp surgical instruments over my husband's body and I could only imagine the machine knocking into the doctor and slicing open my poor husband. Luckily, that didn't happen. I wasn't hurt and managed to do the interpretation, but I was a nervous wreck.

For the next three days, while we stayed at the hospital, I had no time to eat, no place to take a shower, and could barely sleep. Plus, then we had to wait a week for the results of the biopsy. It was torture.

Finally, we went to the doctor's office to hear the results. "Your husband has cancer," the doctor said, "and we will need to remove one of his kidneys, his urethra, and his bladder to stop it from spreading. But even with this surgery, there's no guarantee that it won't appear again."

When my husband heard this news, he wanted a second opinion. He didn't want to lose his job and to be permanently incapacitated by having such essential organs removed. Plus, he was put off by the doctor's arrogance

So, we went to another hospital, but the doctor there told him the same news.

As this was going on, we talked with friends who had in-depth health knowledge and they disagreed with the doctor's opinion. They encouraged him to investigate alternatives.

Not feeling confident in the doctors who had diagnosed him, he made the decision to forego surgery. By this time, I was exhausted, distraught, and deeply worried. I had mixed feelings about my husband's decision, but I loved him and supported him to do what he felt was best.

We were required to go to the hospital yet again to tell the doctor about my husband's decision. The doctor told us that he would be much worse off without surgery and tried his best to convince us that this was the only way.

We proposed just having some simple examinations on a regular basis to monitor the disease, but the doctor said that wasn't possible.

With that, my husband began to take his illness seriously. We got good dietary advice and completely changed what he was eating. I got a water purifier for the faucet in our kitchen. I started buying organic foods, even though they were much more expensive.

A friend suggested I go to a nearby temple and pray. Wanting to be open to every possible means of healing my husband, I went to the temple and prayed—that we would see only the bright side of his condition.

But all of this stress had become too much for me. I started acting erratically. I found myself singing heavy metal songs in the car at the top of my lungs. I'd scrunch up 100s of paper balls and throw them in the corner. I tore apart some textbooks that I should have returned to my employer. My weight dropped from 110 pounds to 88 pounds.

I was a mess.

I talked with my boss, telling him that I couldn't manage to help my husband and do my teaching job at the same time. It was impossible for me to forget about my husband's disease and smile while I was singing and playing with my young students in classes. On top of that, I couldn't control the wild students in my classes and some students quit my classes. I arranged to cut back my hours and work part-time.

Finally, I went to the doctor myself and was diagnosed with an anxiety disorder. The doctor prescribed some Chinese medicine and some Western medicine. The Western medicine made me sick and dizzy, so I had to stop taking it.

Maybe you've had such experience. It seems like when things are going wrong, they all go wrong all at once. Have you noticed that?

I had already been through a great deal in my life. I had dealt with asthma, with operations, with car accidents, and with the terrible relationship between my parents. So, I thought I could handle anything. I was wrong.

But I was able to come through all of these challenges by learning a few fundamental lessons. Apply these in your own life and you will get through whatever challenges may be facing you:

1. **Meditation**: When I was having such a hard time, my husband taught me a simple meditation that helped me come back to peace. Sit down on the floor and close your eyes. Breathe in and out very slowly and smoothly. Just focus on your breath. If negative or disturbing thoughts come into your mind, just bring your attention back to your breath. Once your breath becomes steady and even, imagine you are a boat sailing on the river. Ask yourself, "How fast is the boat

moving, fast or slow? How does it feel?" Now make your decision to continue or change the speed of your boat. It's up to you. You can decide how to live your life.

2. **Give your attention to the core issue first:** For me, the core issue was my job, the two-hour commute, and my need to be there for my husband when he most needed my help. Once I took action, changed to a part-time position working 15 minutes away, then everything changed. What is your core issue? Deal with that first and the rest will come along.

3. **Find the good**: When everything in your life is falling apart, it's easy to think how terrible everything is. But happy people develop a habit of finding the good in any situation. As I began doing that, my whole life changed, and I believe yours will, too.

4. **Get clear on what you want**: This is what The Passion Test teaches: "Clarity is power." Get clear on what you really, deeply care about (your passions), then begin taking steps to make those the priority in your life. When you do that, you'll soon discover that what you want is what you have.

I quit my teaching job six months ago. Now I work just 15 minutes away and it is easy for me to help my husband when he needs me. His health has improved, and I have much more time to be with him. That's what I wanted and that's what I got.

It's hard for me to believe how well things are going now. They were so difficult for so long. But I have a mentor who told me that good things always come after bad.

As I've given priority to things that really matter to me, it's become easier and easier to find the good in life. And the more good I find in life, the more I enjoy my life, and you will, too.

So many people in Japan choose their work just to make a living, not to create a happy life. That's one of the reasons why the suicide rate is so high in my country.

You have a choice. You can choose how fast and what direction your boat will go. Choose well.

Emi Edwards was born into a family of a self-employed car mechanic father and a sewing and knitting mother. From a young age she loved foreign languages and music, teaching herself to speak English. After living overseas, she started to teach English with music and illustrations in Japan. With this, she realized her mission and passion in life: studying and making healing music.

Chapter 18
FROM DARKNESS TO LIGHT . . . DISCOVERING YOUR INNER COMPASS

By Shinoka (Japan)

....

"The darkness in your heart is a gift from the divine God to lead you into the light."

Shinoka, Purity Healer

As I slip under the bedcovers and close my eyes, a single stream of tears pours down my cheek and down the nape of my neck.

The moment I lay down to sleep, after a day at work, my heart overflows in sadness and the tears don't stop.

"Oh, how long will this darkness continue . . ."

The wounded feminine within me quietly spoke somewhere in my heart. It continued to weep for what felt like forever. Sadness put a block in my heart, and I couldn't sleep even if I tried. It was as if darkness was standing close by me, drawing me into the bottomless swamp that is sadness.

"I'm not worthy of love as a woman."

"No one would love me anyway."

My heart suffered as those emotions and beliefs continued to arise in me. I even thought that if I kept crying night after night, I might have a heart attack as I choked on my tears and then this terrible pain would end. This continued for 10 whole years.

If you have ever suffered from a wounded heart, if you've ever felt yourself drowning in sorrow, or if you feel like the darkness enveloping you will never lift, then this chapter is for you. I share my story to give you hope and then I'll give you specific steps you can take right now to remove the pain and suffering forever.

The Death of My Feminine Nature

The trigger that wounded the feminine in me was the time a man rejected our relationship and said: "This is a mistake." He already had a beloved, and I was the other woman—second to her.

In my heart, I felt conflicted that I wasn't his number one, but the limited time that we spent together brought me such peace and joy. The sad reality of it was that I had very low self-esteem and didn't believe that a man could love me the most. So, I allowed myself to be pushed into the shadows as second best. Our relationship never felt completely satisfying, even when we were together. The joy I felt in my heart was constantly at odds with the conflict I felt. Then one day, he ended it all with those words. The background music played through the hollow space where my heart once was, and I followed it into the darkness. I felt as if my femininity was completely denied. I was devastated. With the ending of our romantic relationship, I understood that we had to go back to being friends; however, I was heartbroken over not being accepted as a woman.

Then I became involved with another man. At one point, he pushed me away, laughing and saying, "Don't touch me, ugly woman."

These words felt like sharp arrows shooting right into my heart. My feminine self felt even more hurt, and the belief that no one could love me became more potent. To make sure I would not be wounded again, I quietly closed my heart, but bit by bit I began losing confidence as a woman.

Success Without Love Doesn't Feel Like Success

When I was younger, my masculine energy was strong, and I found it hard to connect with my heart and sexuality as a woman. Even though I looked like a woman, my inner masculinity was so strong that I felt a gap between the two. "I want to live like a normal woman . . . but I don't feel feminine . . ." I cursed myself. So, after I was finally able to open my heart and was met with such devastation, my broken confidence and femininity remained hidden in its shell.

Back then I was a successful career woman, responsible for overseas marketing at Sony and working with embassies from England, Germany, the Middle East, and over 40 countries around the world. After that, I was responsible for corporate communications, creating content for the company's in-house newsletter, writing articles, editing, liaising with the media.

I was at the front line, working successfully on projects that really seemed to matter. I received awards for projects I produced and the articles I wrote appeared in newspapers and magazines. I was asked to be the project leader of an international symposium, which meant that I was organizing an event for over 100 people. I felt confident at work, my bosses had trust in me, and my days were fulfilling.

The conflict in my heart was between the masculine energy that made me successful at work and my feminine nature which yearned to be nurtured and loved.

I loved how I could power through so much work. However, inside, I was unconsciously denying the feminine by not accepting or loving it. One after the other, my friends were getting married and having children, and though I was celebrating how happy they were, deep inside, I was in excruciating pain that said: "I probably will not find my own happiness as a woman."

When did my feminine nature get shut off?

Where It All Started

Deep inside my heart, I kept remembering the words of my beloved mother. My mother was a woman of many talents who enjoyed her life. Later in her life, she became the master of Japanese dancing in the Hanayagi style and performed on stages all over the country. I truly admired how powerful she was, and she made me feel as if there was no such thing as impossible in life. She left this world when I was 33, but the one thing she would always say to me was: "Getting married and having children makes a woman."

Those words ruled over my heart like a curse, and the longer I was single, the more I felt inferior, like I was only half a woman. I worked as hard as possible to find the fulfillment I needed to keep my pain sealed away. To me, my mother was the number-one, most amazing person, who could do anything. And here I was feeling that I was nowhere near her and a failure compared to her. I hid behind my mother's shadow and couldn't accept my own value.

Because of the state of my heart, I ended up attracting relationships that made me hide in someone's shadow, like I was number two, and rather than receive love from men, I allowed myself to be treated negatively. This wounded my tender feminine heart and I felt myself drowning in the darkness of these awful feelings.

Even then people around me would see me as bright and powerful. So, I said to myself, "No one could possibly understand how I truly feel" and my heart split into two conflicting parts—one part for the outside world and one half for my true self.

During the day, I was busy with work, so I didn't have the time to feel pain, but in the evening, the wound in my heart opened up and I couldn't get to sleep. That was also the only time that I could take off my suit of armor to be my true self. My tears helped purify my sadness and set my true self free in that moment.

Two Turning Points

Quite unexpectedly, I arrived at a turning point.

I was still working, but I was also studying the healing arts via a correspondence course on the phone in the evenings. My master sent me healing energy from afar, and the heavy energy that had been weighing me down for a long time was cleansed in a moment. My heart and body felt so much lighter. In that moment I could clearly feel the heavy, dark energy of sadness leave my body and the aura around my heart and body became lighter.

"Is such a magical thing even possible?!" I thought.

With the surprise and shock of it all, I began to study how to heal and read energies from this master.

As I neared graduation, I shared what else I wanted to learn with my master, but he shut me off suddenly saying, "You're impudent." I had just one more step before becoming a healer. Yet again, I plunged back down into the darkness.

That's when I came to the second turning point.

I didn't stay stuck in the darkness for that long.

It happened when I grabbed a stuffed animal—a plush toy dragon.

At that moment, with the strangest beeping sound, I was enveloped in a soft, fluffy energy and I started receiving messages from the invisible world. I experienced that energy as a light being saying to me: "I'm Ryumakura. You don't have to stay in the darkness any longer. Let's live with a soft heart."

September 3, 2000. That was the day I began communicating with the spirit guides in the world of light and, from that day, my life changed 180 degrees for the better.

The master who had shut me off felt my energy soften and we came together again. From another master, I learned how to receive messages from guides from a higher dimension through channeling. I was told multiple times by those guides, "You will heal many from their sadness and pain as the dragon-riding Kannon, also known as Quan Yin (the goddess of compassion)."

That's when I came to the realization that the darkness I had been drowning in from the hurt I inflicted upon myself was vital in my own healing. It turned my heart from darkness to light so I could understand and help others who are suffering. With that realization, the darkness evaporated, as if it had dissolved into mist.

"How loved and celebrated I am by the universe!"

As I began receiving energy and messages from the light beings and Kannon, I began receiving calls for help from people all over Japan and the world. From that I was able to become independent, leaving my career of 23 years at Sony. And as if I was being led by the hand, I began working as a heart-healing healer and a messenger of Kannon's love, light, and compassion. At times, other healers would refer those with deep darkness within them to me. As I came out of my hard-working job at Sony into serving the light and my life turned around 180 degrees, I realized:

"Wow, the outside and inside of my heart have united."

"How good it feels to not have any conflict in my heart!"

"Energy and abundance flow through my body smoothly and without blockage!"

From my experience of having a two-layered, conflicted heart, I could hear the true voice of my clients who weren't necessarily telling me the whole truth. And if I just send light to the armor they're using to protect themselves, the light destroys the armor and provides healing, which in turn transforms their energy to something much softer. As I sent out pure light to them, at the same time, I was also healing more and more.

When you truly feel that you are loved by the universe, everything turns around for the better. Even though I don't work as intensely as I did at Sony, by trusting the flow of light, abundance began to circulate. I started a Goddess Academy, where I support people who have rejected their feminine or are limiting themselves from living authentically. I help them cleanse the darkness and remove the limitations that prevent them from living more freely. The connection I have with the light continues to deepen as I heal more and more. I have experienced so much synchronicity as both my work and relationships continue to improve.

Based on my own experiences, let me share a few steps you can use to turn your life around too.

1. **Don't run away from the pain (fear, sadness) of your past.** Heal the pain in your heart and the relationships you have with others. Negative emotions are an important key to finding the light ahead. Without denying past pain, find the cause of the pain. By healing it inside yourself using a tool like The Work of Byron Katie, you can forgive someone with whom you are angry. That will free your mind and improve your energy flow. Ask yourself: "Is this true? Why do I think the other person acted that way? What is the gift of this experience? What can I do to heal myself and forgive the other person?" When you realize that the painful feeling that you have long held was created by your own thoughts, your relationship with others will change. The key is to find the light that's at the end of that negative emotion. Don't seal away the pain and, instead, heal the cause and forgive the other person. This will liberate your heart and the flow of your energy will improve.

2. **Take off your suit of armor and accept your true feelings without conflict.** "How does my heart feel? Is that what I truly want to do? Am I trying to please somebody else's expectation?" Ask your heart these questions. Tell yourself "I'm fine as who I am" and accept your authentic self. By accepting negative emotions and being honest about how you truly feel, your self-trust will begin to grow.

3. **Have a childlike curiosity and playfulness and connect with innocence, that is also purity.** Spend time in nature. Take action to do whatever will bring joy to your heart. Don't think twice. Enjoy it like a child. Try to keep this in mind during your day-to-day life. Playfulness is a state of innocence. When you're playful like a child, your heart will be purified, and it will become easier to receive energy from the source of the universe.

4. **Make choices from your purest feelings and never from your ego.** Ask your heart: "Is this decision coming from my ego? Am I choosing from a place of pure love?" Your ego tends to try to protect itself and get defensive. When you make choices from a place of pure love, your relationships will improve.

5. **Let go of conscious thought, let your mind become empty like the sky and connect with your higher self.** Meditate for 20 minutes every day, whenever is best for you day or night. Your mind tries to find an answer through your past experiences. By emptying your mind through meditation, you're able to open up your intuition and receive divine wisdom. I will share how to meditate later on.

6. **Trust your intuition and flow with the guidance of light to lead your life.** Relax your body and let go of tension. Do things to slow down: have a bath, take a walk, or listen to comforting music.

When you have these things in your awareness, it'll become easier to listen to your intuition. When you receive inspiration, turn it into action as soon as possible. By trusting the experiences in your life, your inner navigational system, your intuition will begin to move and the path to your highest good will naturally open up.

As a practical exercise to help you implement those 6 steps, let me share a self-cleansing meditation to connect with your truest self.

- Find a time in the morning or night and a quiet place you can be alone. Dim the lights in your room and sit on a chair.
- Imagine a cord coming out from your tail bone, connecting to the center of the earth. This is your grounding cord.
- Close your eyes and breathe slowly and deeply.
- Imagine a ball of light above your head.
- Imagine that with each breath in, the ball of light moves through your body from the crown chakra at the top of your head.
- This ball is a sparkling, shining golden light. Imagine this light spreading through your body, cleansing any negativity in your thoughts, emotions, and cells.
- Imagine that with each breath out, any fear, worry, past anger, and other negative emotions leave your body and are released into the center of the earth.
- After breathing like this for a while, empty your mind and bring focus to your heart center. Continue to meditate within that silence.
- When the time comes to an end, take a deep breath and slowly open your eyes.

By doing meditations like this for 20 minutes every day, your heart will feel more peaceful. Once you're used to meditating, you can begin to release any particular events that you've been stuck on.

You can also imagine your heart always being at peace and send a pink light to your heart center too as pink is the color of love.

My past experiences were vital in discovering my hidden talents and true purpose in life. As deep as my darkness was, like yin and yang, when it flipped, I was able to use that to transform it into light.

Now I love my femininity fully. The mist that cloaked my heart is clear and there is no longer a struggle with the masculinity within me. These experiences have allowed me to now help those who suffer from being unable to accept their own femininity, those who have been hurt as women, those who are worried or afraid to be loved, and those who continue to work hard using their masculine energy and denying their own femininity. As their hearts and emotions heal, I support them to return to their original sacred woman and connect with the goddess within them.

If you are having challenges with people or have pain from the past, please do not give up. Know that there is meaning to everything you experience in this life. Even if it seems like a negative experience, know that it is a gift from God for you to discover the light that is within you. Face your pain and suffering instead of running away, and when you peel off the veil of darkness, little by little, you'll begin to see your purest self. There your talents and true purpose are hidden. The key is to learn to love and heal yourself.

When you have begun healing, even if you don't try hard, your life will begin to flow in a happier direction. You are always protected by light. When you begin walking the path of your soul's true purpose, you will become a powerful being, with the guides of light cheering you on and however you may serve this world, they will celebrate you for bringing more light onto this earth.

Shinoka is a Purity Healer and Coach, both in Japan and around the world, who brings healing and transformation of the soul to her clients. At one time she was in charge of Sony Corporation's overseas marketing division and responsible for several hundred million yen in business with embassies and broadcasting stations in more than 40 countries overseas. After working for 23 years in this role, she was put in charge of editing in-house newsletters and responding to media reports as a public relations officer. In 2004, Shinoka opened healing room Sophia in Yokohama, Japan. As a healer, channeler, counselor, manager, seminar leader, and author, she has now consulted with more than 10,000 clients. Fusing "spirituality" and "business," Shinoka teaches the laws of the universe that draw richness, how to refine intuition, and how to use the energy of the invisible world. In 2010, she opened Sophia Goddess School, which helps women heal their feminine essence, connecting with the purity inside, and so that each woman is able to shine like herself. Trained as Foster Rainbow Wheel Instructor®, Purity Healer, and Purity Coach, she now trains certified facilitators to hold courses in Japan and overseas. As a marketing coach, Passion Test, and Passion Test for Business consultant, she also supports entrepreneurs and managers. Shinoka combines Kannon's energy and business. She brings healing and transformation of the soul, conveying the way of life that combines the world of light with creating real money and abundance through online courses and the Happy & Abundance Club Online Salon.

Chapter 19
THE POWER OF WORDS TO TRANSFORM HEARTACHE INTO JOY

By Marron Hoshino (Japan)

· ·

"Our inner words can change the world—transmuting sadness into energy."

—Marron Hoshino

One morning, my husband hadn't appeared to walk the dog at the usual time. So, I went to our bedroom, only to find him, collapsed on the bed. His eyes were wide open, yet he was completely unconscious. I immediately called an ambulance and we were soon at the hospital, with its white corridors and antiseptic smells.

The emergency doctor who examined him ordered an MRI and that was how I learned he had a brain hemorrhage. The doctor ordered immediate surgery, but right before surgery, he came to me with a solemn expression on his face, "We may save his life but there's a high likelihood he will not fully recover."

As the doctor was speaking to me, I had the most curious experience. While I looked up at the doctor, listening to his words, I was conscious of also feeling as if my awareness was hovering over my own head, listening to the doctor's words from up near the ceiling. That version of myself said: "It's okay to not believe him. I can help my husband walk again. He will climb up and down the stairs."

With that encouragement, I visualized my husband going up and down our stairs and ingrained that into the back of my mind. It was the beginning of a very long fight. Though the operation went well, there were so many cords attached to his body as he lay in bed, unconscious, that I couldn't help but blankly stare at the man who was supposedly my husband.

In this chapter, I'll share the remarkable journey my husband and I took together and how this tragedy was transformed into a great blessing in my life. There were some key lessons I learned through this experience. In sharing them with you, I hope it may make it possible for you to find the strength and hope to move through the tragedies in your own life.

A brain hemorrhage is a terrible thing. This man who was talking and eating just yesterday lost his ability to talk, eat, or walk in the blink of an eye. Once his brain activity collapsed, his hands and feet didn't work any longer. It was impossible for him to get up out of bed, and, as a result, he lay in that bed for days and days.

First, to realize my vision of my husband walking, I took whatever action I could. I was only allowed to spend 20 minutes with him three times a day in the ICU after the surgery because his condition was so delicate. During these times, I massaged his hands and feet with the hope that this would help with any of the after-effects of his surgery.

While he was unconscious, I gave him updates on his two beloved black shiba dogs to help him reconnect with something he loved. I had heard that even in a coma, the subconscious is still listening.

The taste of the curry we had together the day before he collapsed felt so far in the distance. It triggered the thought that we might never eat together again, and I felt how lucky it is to just to be normal and happy. Whenever I'd wake at night, I would be overwhelmed with sadness and the morning would arrive as I laid in the emptiness of his loss.

The worst of his recovery was during Christmas. I would dream of my husband, who could no longer speak, wishing me Merry Christmas.

But I decided to accept that he was seriously ill. I made the conscious decision to accept my sadness, to not look away from the situation, and to face it head-on. I wanted my husband to walk again, so I found a hospital that had a reputation for being very good at rehabilitation. When they couldn't help him anymore, we then went to another hospital, and for two and a half years, we continued to rehabilitate his body. If I found a good alternative therapy, I would get permission to take him out of the hospital. Then I went the distance to find ways to help overcome the effects of his brain hemorrhage. I spoke to all kinds of people and experts about how to help him, and then I did what they told me.

After a while, I began to feel that rather than losing my husband, he was giving my soul a chance to shine. The sudden change in our relationship made me feel so grateful for even the smallest things.

I realized that this tragedy with my husband had allowed me to see what was most important to me. By carefully tending to those things that are most important, you can find where you belong and begin a cycle of joy.

I was able to find joy in the changes in my husband's state. The biggest change within me was that I stopped going after the result of my husband being able to walk perfectly. Even if he couldn't walk again, I realized that there is so much precious value in his existence and his life. No matter what the result, I arrived at a place where each day brought happiness to me and I could feel joy all the time. I was no longer looking at my husband's illness as a negative—I was strong, yet soft and flexible.

In the ancient native Japanese language of Yamato-Kotoba, this is expressed with the word "Taoyaka." This word supported me throughout the heaviest period of my husband's illness. It means that no matter how heavy the winter snow falls onto the bamboo, it will take the weight without ever breaking, and when the snow is ready to melt, the bamboo actually flings the snow off itself and returns to its original, straight form.

The word "Taoyaka" describes the human heart that can also be strong, yet soft and flexible like the bamboo. I love this word. As my husband fought for his life, by holding the state of "Taoyaka" in my heart, no matter how much I wanted to cry and fall apart, I could stay light and flexible.

Words are energy, and energy creates reality. In Japan, there's a type of faith that believes in Kotodama, and our belief is that words have Spirit within them that can transform reality. So, if you chant a word that you want to create a particular effect, it can have a positive influence on your experience. Words can cheer up a person in such a powerful way and become the power that turns your vision into reality. The reason I could stay optimistic throughout my husband's recovery was because I relied on the power of words.

"It's okay. He will get better. How joyous. I'm happy." I repeated words that made me strong, yet soft and flexible, so I could change my world to be full of joy. I said these words in my heart, as well as out loud. Both were effective.

Happiness isn't something for the future. It doesn't come from something great happening, or having something wonderful, but it comes from somewhere deep inside. When we connect with that happiness, then our happiness is unconditional. I realized this during my husband's recovery. It wasn't that I would become happy because he got better. Even when he was at his worst, my husband continuously gave his soul's shining, positive energy to me.

I learned that the important thing when someone falls ill is to maintain your authentic power and to not be shaken up by circumstances. Feeling negative about the illness is just a matter of perspective. Illness is an important gift that reminds us of the true brightness of one's soul.

When we live true to the love that is within us, we are able to accept things unconditionally without labelling something as good, bad, positive, or negative. We can simply feel joy in each moment. Feeling joy in everything is the ultimate happiness. I discovered that sadness, joy, feeling every type of emotion found in life must be what happiness is.

As my husband overcame the after-effects of the brain hemorrhage and his disability became less and less, I could feel that my own energy was delivered to him as light, which he would reflect back to me. There was a harmonic cycle of light flowing between us.

Then, one day, he suddenly said, "Thanks." I will never forget the happiness I felt that day. There were so many small joys during his recovery. When he walked by himself without his cane . . . when he drank water out of the cup on his own . . . when he finally said "Merry Christmas" to me after a year . . . the moment he reunited with his beloved dogs, Kumi and Kuma . . . each scene was life's greatest gift, the memories of which still give me so much to this day.

A person who is clear on what is important to them is a happy person. Life becomes fulfilled with inner joy, happiness, and fun by carefully gathering everything that is important to us and growing it.

Janet Attwood, the founder of The Passion Test, which transforms the world through love, says: "Get clear on what is most important to you, and by living for it with passion you are able to create the most amazing life full of love and joy."

In my case, by standing by my husband through his recovery and quietly pouring in my passion for his return to health, I was able to realize that happiness was everywhere, and I found joy in every little thing. There is much sadness that comes with life. But by facing that sadness with courage, you'll find that sadness is connected to everything that is beautiful in this world. The world is made of a strong energy of love that only comes from overcoming sadness.

When we fully feel sadness, our hearts are cleansed, and this leads to a very transparent, open, vulnerable feeling. That feeling of vulnerability is like a spring, and when you face sadness despite the pain and arrive at the very bottom of it, you can then allow loving energy to lead you to happiness.

It is this loving energy that allows us to have the strength to keep moving forward.

Sadness, out of all human emotions, is the most beautiful thing—like a transparent lake. You may feel deeply for someone and feel sadness. But going beyond that sadness to the joy that lies underneath it—that is power. That is love and it connects us to the path of hope.

One day, three and a half years or so after that day when I floated above my body knowing that I didn't have to believe the doctors, the vision of my husband climbing up and down the stairs at home came true. I experienced the very scene of my earlier vision of him climbing up and down the stairs with my support. I will never forget how I felt that day.

When you are faced with something that feels impossible, it is important to have a clear vision of what you want to be possible. And the energy that makes that vision a reality is the power of "Kotodama" (the spirit of words). By using your own words of support as energy, your dreams can come true. It can be as simple as "It's okay." By repeating that amazing, supportive word over and over in your heart, your life will transform into something as amazing as that word. I will guarantee this.

No matter how hard times get, it's important to believe that the world is beautiful. Within you, you have such powerful love that transmutes sadness into energy and energy into action. By acting out of that deep love, you can overcome any devastating adversities and the belief of "I can't take it."

You can use your powerful inner words to transform your life into something spectacular. No matter how hard it is right now, how sunken you are in sadness, that sadness will change into something full of joy, and you'll live through such fun, beautiful days in time. You can overcome this. Just hold your favorite words that give you courage, and a clear vision of your desired future, somewhere deep in your heart and take passionate action. Your inner light will make your dreams come true.

I dedicate this poem to you with the belief that you will overcome sadness and become joy itself, that the flower of light within you will bloom in time . . .

"The Universe in the Light of White Lilies"
By Marron Hoshino

Girls,
Even though you can't see the truth
But I can see
Around your breast
There are small white lilies' buds
which are crouching, longing for the future
They are knitting their future slowly

They are folding soft, transparent petals
They are preparing to give out sweet perfume
in the morning garden someday
as if they were counting on their wedding day.

White lilies have good manners
Even if there are many buds on each stem,
They never compete with another for blooming at one time
One of them blooms; after waiting for a few days,
Then another lily opens slowly

When the first lily drops its petals,
Another lily is coming into flower quietly again

There is an invisible clock designed on a transparent crystal
It always keeps the order of the universe
And all lilies are definitely coming out
There is no lily that will give up its blooming
Even small buds come into flower strongly
until the last has bloomed

If you can see each petal of the lilies in the sun,
They're the incarnation of light with their shining flower heart.

Girls,
May your longing be like sweet beautiful perfume someday
Believe the force of the lily in your heart
And then you will keep the order of the universe
Bloom in your flower gently, exaltedly
Bloom in yourself,
in your longing
The life of the flower named you
Shine in the light forever

If you have a difficulty in your life,
Please remember
in your heart
There is a white lily blooming
No matter who takes it from you by force

Somewhere in the universe
There is the shore of light
In every season, I heard, a transparent white lily is blooming

From the shore,
At the edge of the universe,
I wish from the bottom of my heart
every girl in the world,
even if they become old, are tired of their life
They will come back to their gentle whiteness of the lily,
Honestly.

Marron Hoshino is a poet and poetry reader and a Noh journalist. Born at the foot of Mt. Fuji, she began reading and writing poetry as a teen. In her twenties, she began reciting improvisational poems in Berlin and other galleries around the world. In 1997, she received the "DNA of Poetry Award" from the World Poet Conference in England. Her poem, titled, "An Elegy for the Millenium" was awarded special recognition by Japan's Ministry of Education and Science in 2015. For her work in igniting Japanese interest in poetry and reviving interest in the traditional Japanese performing art called "Noh," in 2016 Marron received the Prince Higashikyunomiya Culture Prize. Actively involved in Japanese writing and poetry circles, she has a deep belief in the miraculous power of the ancient language of Japan, "Yamato Kotoba." The poetry of this ancient language has a reputation for reaching deep into people's souls, giving them peace of mind, and providing encouragement and courage. You can enjoy her poetry and reach her through her website, "Abundant Gifts from The Poetry Forests" by searching for Marron Hoshino.

EPILOGUE

Isn't it amazing how many things we share with others all around the world? We hope that these stories have opened your eyes and helped you to see that you're not alone.

The next step is to put what you've learned into practice. Find those stories and the recommendations of the authors that most resonate with you. Then try out what they suggest. See what works and what doesn't. Not every practice will be right for you, but we're sure that buried within these pages are at least one or two that will change your life.

Thank you for taking this journey with us. When you bought this book, you gained access to a collection of free gifts from the authors in this book. If you haven't yet collected yours, you can get them here:

www.thedoortoinnerhappiness.com

If you enjoyed this book and gained value from it, please share it with others, and let us know how your life is changing. You can reach us at: support@thepassiontest.com.

With our love and gratitude,

Janet and Chris

A free ebook edition is available with the purchase of this book.

To claim your free ebook edition:

Visit MorganJamesBOGO.com
Sign your name CLEARLY in the space
Complete the form and submit a photo of
the entire copyright page
You or your friend can download the ebook
to your preferred device

Morgan James BOGO™

A **FREE** ebook edition is available for you
or a friend with the purchase of this print book.

CLEARLY SIGN YOUR NAME ABOVE

Instructions to claim your free ebook edition:
1. Visit MorganJamesBOGO.com
2. Sign your name CLEARLY in the space above
3. Complete the form and submit a photo
   of this entire page
4. You or your friend can download the ebook
   to your preferred device

Print & Digital Together Forever.

Snap a photo

Free ebook

Read anywhere

CPSIA information can be obtained
at www.ICGtesting.com
Printed in the USA
JSHW042326140421
13582JS00001B/38